# THE ARTFUL POSE



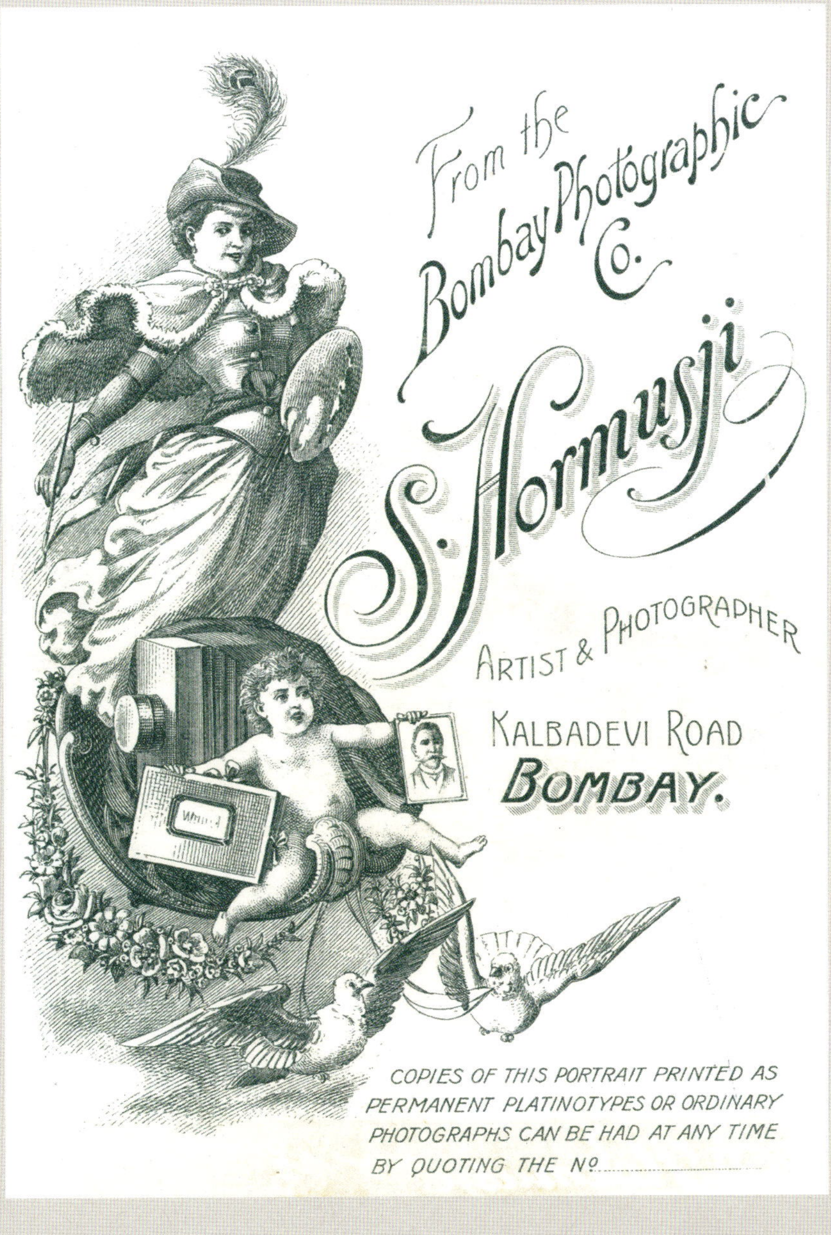

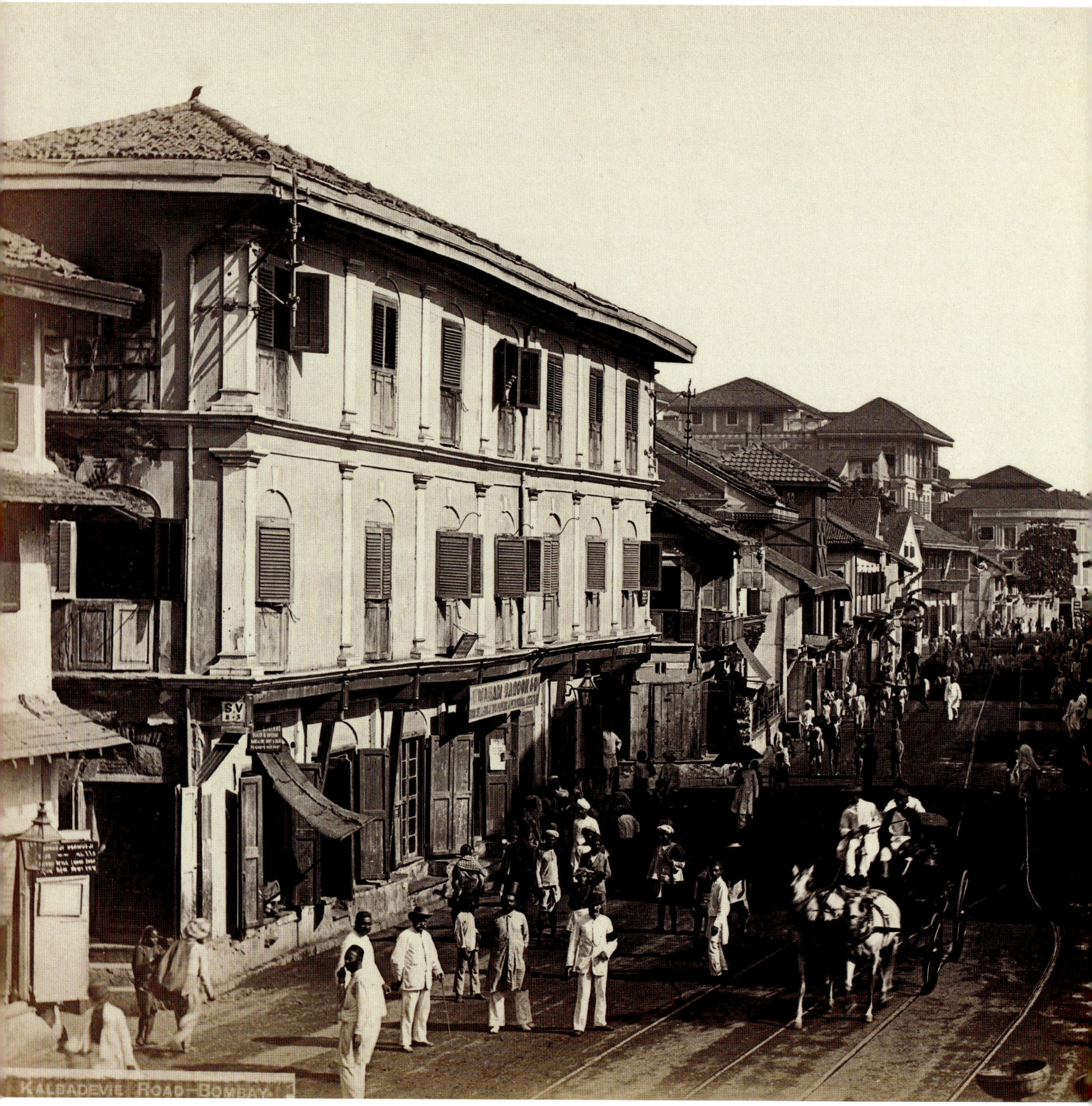

KALBADEVIE ROAD—BOMBAY.

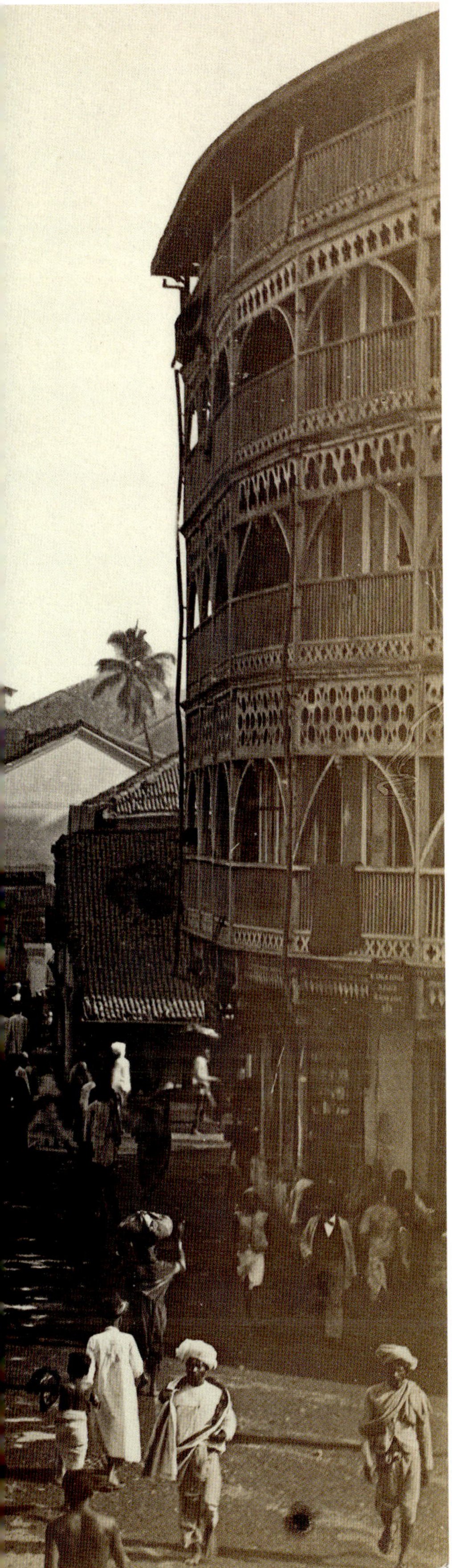

# THE ARTFUL POSE

## EARLY STUDIO PHOTOGRAPHY IN MUMBAI

c. 1855–1940


CONTRIBUTORS

Prof. Partha Mitter

Akshaya Tankha

Suryanandini Sinha

Rahaab Allana

With a Foreword by

Tasneem Zakaria Mehta



The Alkazi Collection of Photography
NEW DELHI • LONDON • NEW YORK

DR. BHAU DAJI LAD
MUMBAI CITY MUSEUM

Mapin Publishing
AHMEDABAD

This catalogue is published in conjunction with the exhibition
*The Artful Pose: Early Studio Photography in Mumbai (c. 1855–1940)*
held from 28 February–21 March 2010 at
Dr. Bhau Daji Lad Mumbai City Museum, Mumbai

First published in India in 2010 by
Mapin Publishing Pvt. Ltd
in association with
Dr. Bhau Daji Lad Mumbai City Museum
and
The Alkazi Collection of Photography

Simultaneously published in the
United States of America in 2010 by
Grantha Corporation
77 Daniele Drive, Hidden Meadows
Ocean Township, NJ 07712
E: mapin@mapinpub.com
and
The Alkazi Collection of Photography
India: New Delhi | rahaab@acparchives.com
United Kingdom: London | stephanie.roy@btinternet.com

Mapin Publishing Pvt. Ltd
502 Paritosh, Near Darpana Academy
Usmanpura Riverside, Ahmedabad 380 013 INDIA
T: +91 79 40 228 228 | F: +91 79 40 228 201
E: mapin@mapinpub.com | www.mapinpub.com

Dr. Bhau Daji Lad Mumbai City Museum
Veer Mata Jijabai Bhonsale Udyan, 91/A Dr. Ambedkar Road
Byculla East, Mumbai 400 027 INDIA
T: +91 22 23731234 / 65560394
E: bdlmuseum@gmail.com | www.bdlmuseum.org

The Alkazi Collection of Photography
M–141, Greater Kailash II
New Delhi 110 048 INDIA
T: +91 11 4143 7426 / 7427
www.acparchives.com



ISBN: 978-81-89995-40-9 (Mapin)
ISBN: 978-1-935677-00-0 (Grantha)
LCCN: 2010923060

Editor: Vinutha Mallya | Mapin Editorial
Design: Paulomi Shah | Mapin Design Studio
Processed at Reproscan, Mumbai
Printed at Thomson Press, Mumbai

COVER:
SHAPOOR N. BHEDWAR,
*Tyag No. 4 – The Mystic Sign*
carbon print, c. 1890s. See p. 68–69

PAGE 1:
S. HORMUSJI, BOMBAY PHOTOGRAPHIC CO.
Verso of Cabinet Card, 165 x 107 mm,
c. 1880–1890 [The Alkazi Collection of Photography]

PAGES 2–3:
E. TAURINES (POSSIBLY)
'Kalbadevie Road—Bombay',
albumen silver print, 185 x 230 mm,
c. 1880s [ACP: 99.16.0002]

# Contents

# Foreword

*The Artful Pose: Early Studio Photography in Mumbai (c. 1855–1940)* is the first important exhibition to be held at the Dr. Bhau Daji Lad Mumbai City Museum since its opening in January 2008. It is an honour for the Museum to collaborate with the Alkazi Foundation for the Arts to showcase this important collection in Mumbai for the first time. The exhibition evolved from the exciting idea of holding a show of early studio photographs in the precinct of the Museum, whose unique collection of models and dioramas speaks precisely to the tradition that these photographs embody.

The exhibition takes a commanding art-historical view of developments in photography, which had closely mirrored developments in painting, taught at colonial art schools at the time. Like the Museum's collection, which was the direct result of art school teaching and production, early studio photography borrowed much in composition, from both painting and theatre. The early-twentieth century was an exciting period of technological advances and the changes it wrought on peoples lives were dramatic. The camera and printing processes comprehensively changed the way images were produced and consumed. The ordinary man who could never have afforded a painted portrait previously, could, with the advent of the camera, present nuanced portraits of himself to the world. Photographs were tableaux of everyday lives, and they became powerful tools for acquisition of knowledge about people and places and a means of controlling and manipulating perceptions.

The exhibition is a first for many more reasons. It presents the work of Narayan Daji, the brother of the Museum's founding father, Dr. Bhau Daji Lad, for the first time. His portrayals of ordinary people are deeply evocative even though they conform to colonial requirements. There is a regal dignity in these portraits of the local people. It is the first time, as well, that the work of Shapoor N. Bhedwar is being presented in Mumbai. An accomplished photographer, he aspired to elevate the art of photography to that of painting. Each image has a lyrical, poetic quality that enshrines a moment. Light and composition are used for dramatic effect.

The exhibition also showcases some of the earliest photomontages from the two-volume *The Oriental Races and Tribes, Residents and Visitors of Bombay* by William Johnson. In addition, there are cartes-de-viste and portraits of Parsi school girls and gentlemen that recall the paintings of early artists of J.J. School of Art, like M.F. Pithawala and M.V. Durandhar, who are represented in the Museum's collection.

In the Museum's "Origins of Mumbai Gallery", we have presented a small collection of photographs of the city rarely seen before. Mumbai's early architectural history forms a compelling narrative aside to the main focus of the exhibition. Many of the studios were located in the streets and by-lanes presented in the photographs here. It becomes almost impossible to recognise the city then from the clutter and chaos of the city now. But a few vignettes of the past remain, like some of the studios mentioned in the essays.

The exhibition retells history both as reality and as fantasy, drawing the viewer into another world. The catalogue that accompanies the exhibition has fascinating insights by eminent scholars on this world, its motivations, its references and its compulsions. It presents the history of not only early photography, but also of the nineteenth and early-twentieth centuries.

**Tasneem Zakaria Mehta**
Managing Trustee and Honorary Director
Dr. Bhau Daji Lad Mumbai City Museum

# A Curatorial Note

Mumbai, at the water's edge, is a metaphor for hard-earned opportunities, looking towards the horizon at the future of an entire nation. Lining India's vast mid-western shoreline lies a heaving metropolis, entranced by prospects of trade and commerce, yet equally dwelling on the nuanced infusions of religion, industry and the vision of Indian cinema. Mumbai is one of India's most distinct frontiers, where people from across the shores have come to share their cultures and often found a home. And so, in this racially diverse, shimmering harbour city, where grand gothic buildings shelter the incredible humanity, lies the core of the exhibition, namely, the extraordinary people and photographers of Mumbai [erstwhile Bombay].

The earliest images in the exhibition are by Narayan Daji, from 1855, whose poignant contribution finds its way to his brother Dr. Bhau Daji Lad's namesake institution, earlier, the Victoria and Albert Museum. The fascinating ethnography of Mumbai unfurls through the rich contours of society, its residents, labourers, castes and communities, enduring through the resilient eye of the lens, creating layered biographies through time and tempting buried memories to the fore. These silver testimonials were taken by a succession of photographers who travelled extensively in Asia and abroad, pointing their powerful lens across continents, allowing them to transgress the bounds of their own regional or national identity. Hence, the exhibition is as much about an encounter with time as about transcending the contexts it presents; as much about engaging with reality on the ground, as about ideologically breaking norms; about those dividing lines that may define place and race, as it is about crossing those thresholds to embrace a renewed identity.

Mumbai took to photography as early as 1840. The more artistic and theatrical elements found a convivial space here, revealed through a barrage of early studio photographs by local and Parsi practitioners. Early endeavours of the camera in India were directed at capturing ceremonial aspects of courtly life, the landscape and ethnography. Having viewed many such images, perhaps the outward effect was to provoke the human desire to be elsewhere and to be transported through a photographic format. Images enabled a twin identity, creating an imaginary space that could be circulated—privately, publicly and conceptually—while feeding and sustaining that illusory entity called the "self".

Mumbai became one of the largest centres of photography's patronage and dispersal in India between the mid-nineteenth and early-twentieth century. The exhibition begins with a keen recording of native castes and tribes, that in time gradually expands to the experimentation with portraiture, performance and popular art in numerous photo studios such as S. Hormusji, Shapoor N. Bhedwar, Bombay Photo Company and EOS Photographic Co. among others. By the late-nineteenth century, professionals and independent firms, such as Bourne & Shepherd and Lala Deen Dayal & Sons, would enlarge the ambit of photography's influence as a widespread democratic medium, with enduring images of families, official and personal leather-bound souvenir albums, carte-de-visite portraits and even the city, exposed as a rising industrial metropolis.

The core themes in this exhibition therefore address the mixtures, fusions and collaborations that were developed during the late-nineteenth century, and how they were re-divided into new categories in the twentieth century. It happened to objects like photographs, which when displaced or dispersed were put under new headings in new hands. It happened to the people in photographs, who when they changed countries, took on new identities; that when dressed, as we see in the exhibition, in the graceful vestiges of a yogi, a courtier, or a woman in a bedchamber, found solace and freedom in photography's refreshingly liberal and experimental tendency.

And so, it is indeed through these photographs that we may be drawn to express our own fragile, latent yet conscious and intimate connections with the past.

**Rahaab Allana**
Curator
Alkazi Foundation for the Arts

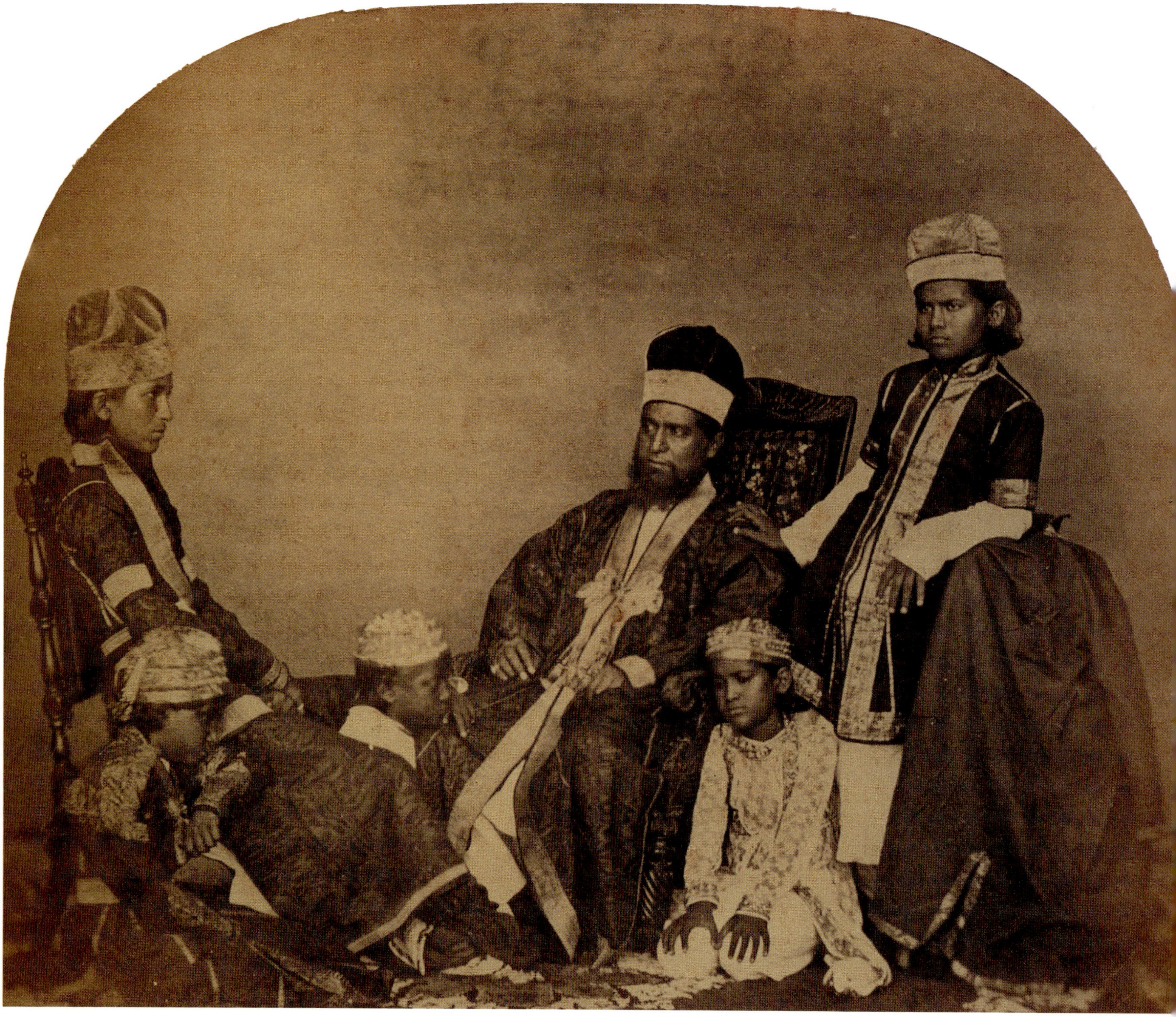

# The Dawn of Photography in India
## A Complex Legacy of the Photographic Studio

Prof. Partha Mitter

Early photography in India, practiced both inside and outside the studio, offers us a fascinating social history of its patronage and usage, underscoring the need for a deeper investigation of the challenges the new medium faced and changes it wrought in visual culture. While the thrust of my paper is an investigation into the pictorial conventions adapted by the early photographers, I will pay particular attention to one aspect of its history: the rise of the posed studio photograph.

I propose a bold hypothesis here that there is a connection between photography—a product of modern technology—and the courtly art of the great Mughals who belonged to the pre-industrial era. This may seem somewhat surprising at first but, as I hope to show, there are indeed some unexpected connections between these two seemingly disparate subjects.[1]

By the nineteenth century, even as modern technology and other accoutrements of the British Empire had virtually obliterated Mughal courtly culture, traces of that culture survived through the modern device of photography (Fig. 1). The failure of the Great Uprising of 1857 dealt a deathblow to Mughal culture as the last Mughal emperor was banished to distant Burma. The industrial revolution transformed the East India Company from a trading outpost to a vast modern territory, held together by a wide network of railways and fast communication system, such as the telegraph. The new contraption called the "camera" seemed to epitomise the unshaken faith in technology that marked the Victorian Era.[2] With the arrival of the camera in the subcontinent in the 1840s, photographic societies sprang up in the presidency towns of India, namely Bombay, Madras and Calcutta [now Mumbai, Chennai and Kolkata respectively], mostly dominated by Europeans. But, as the visual anthropologist Christopher Pinney points out, of the 100 members of the Photographic Society of Bengal, some 30 were Indian.[3]

### Photography's Early Encounters with India

The period was one of lively experiments but early on there was a growing cleavage between amateurs and professionals. Today only a few works can be identified with certainty from that period. The leading Bengali historian Rajendralal Mitra was a member of the first photographic society of India and one of the earliest Indian amateurs to take up photography but we do not know what kind of photographs he took.[4] On the other hand, we have the works of Narayan Daji,

FIG. 1 | UNKNOWN PHOTOGRAPHER
***Moghuls, Mussulmans, of Royal Family of Delhi***
albumen silver print, 135 x 153 mm, c. 1864–1869, from *People of India* series, Vol. 4 (1869), text by Col. Meadows Taylor
[ACP: D2005.88.0004 (24)]

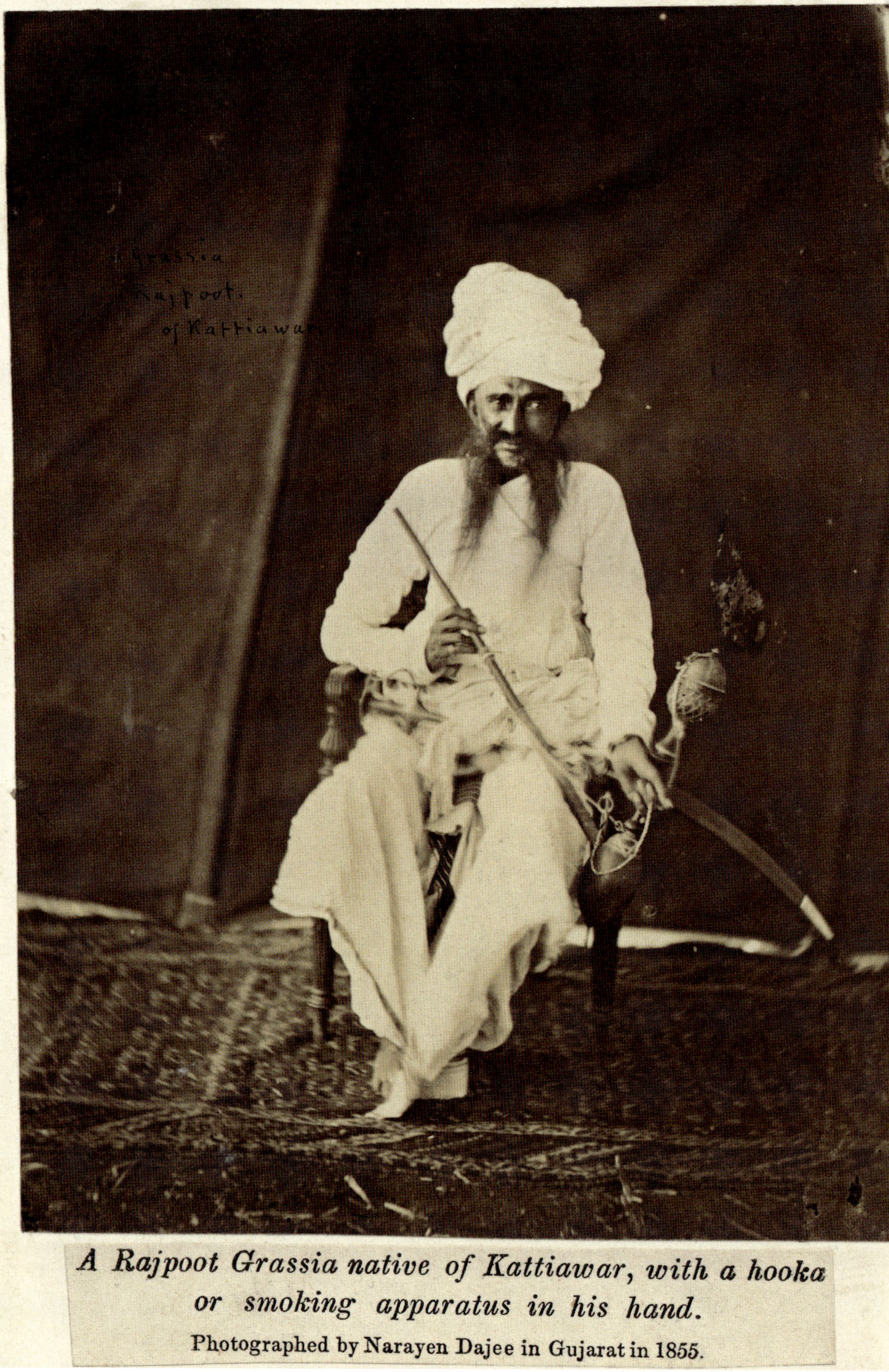

***A Rajpoot Grassia native of Kattiawar, with a hooka or smoking apparatus in his hand.***

Photographed by Narayen Dajee in Gujarat in 1855.

a medical doctor from Bombay, and brother of the well known Indologist Dr. Bhau Daji. Dr. Narayan Daji showed two ethnographic works at the Photographic Society of Bombay in 1855—the Bohra cultivators of Gujarat and a Girasia Rajput tribal from Kathiawar [now part of Gujarat] (Fig. 2). These were highly acclaimed for their technical precision and aesthetic appeal.[5]

Early Indian photographers were keen to keep up with the innovations in the West, and none more so than the Bombay photographer, Shapoor N. Bhedwar. In 1982, while I was researching the exhibition *Photography in India—1858–1980*, I first came across this obscure photographer from Bombay. Bhedwar showed two of his works at the Crystal Palace in London c. 1889, which were praised for technical accomplishment and artistic taste. These two are from his opulent volume called *Art Studies*, dating from 1890s, consisting of 31 carbon prints. They are self-consciously artistic works that drew upon Victorian painting in their lighting, composition and arrangement of figures. Bhedwar leapt to fame within a year with his series called "The Feast of Roses", carrying away the coveted gold medal of the Royal Photographic Society (Fig. 3). In 1891, his work was praised by none other than Henry Peach Robinson, father of the movement known as Pictorialism. Bhedwar was the only non-European to be admitted to Robinson's Linked Ring Brotherhood.[6]

In his intimate indoor scenes Prince Samarendra Chandra Deb Barman of Tripura followed the trend in later Pictorialism that prevailed from the 1890s to the Great War of 1914. I quote Peter Bunnell here on the movement:

> "More and more photographers turned from the depiction of the world around them to the portrayal of personal sentiments and emotions. They focussed their cameras on intimate spaces and close-up details … and a lack of real depth in the pictorial space became a characteristic of works where the photographer sought to draw attention to the difference between traditional, three dimensional optical rendering and the newer, flattened space created within the work itself."[7]

The representation of the third dimension in photography was of course a European convention rather than Indian. It would be tempting to say that Deb Barman was influenced by post-Mughal visual language. In fact, he was arguably more influenced by the soft modelling of Edwardian painting than late Mughal miniatures.

However, when one turns to commercial photography, one is struck by the fact that Indian and non-Indian photographers shared certain approaches commensurate with the available technology. Darogha Abbas Ali, a municipal engineer with the colonial government in Lucknow, was the photographer who replaced the pioneering "Chhote Miyan" in popularity. His highly popular work, *The Lucknow Album*, was published in 1870. The album called *The Beauties of Lucknow*, dated 1855, is also attributed to Abbas Ali[8] (Fig. 4a–b). These courtesans have an endearing candidness in their pose.

FIG. 2 | NARAYAN DAJI
*A Rajpoot Grassia native of Kattiawar, with a hooka or smoking apparatus in his hand*
albumen silver print, 1855
[ACP: 2005.01.0001 (15)]

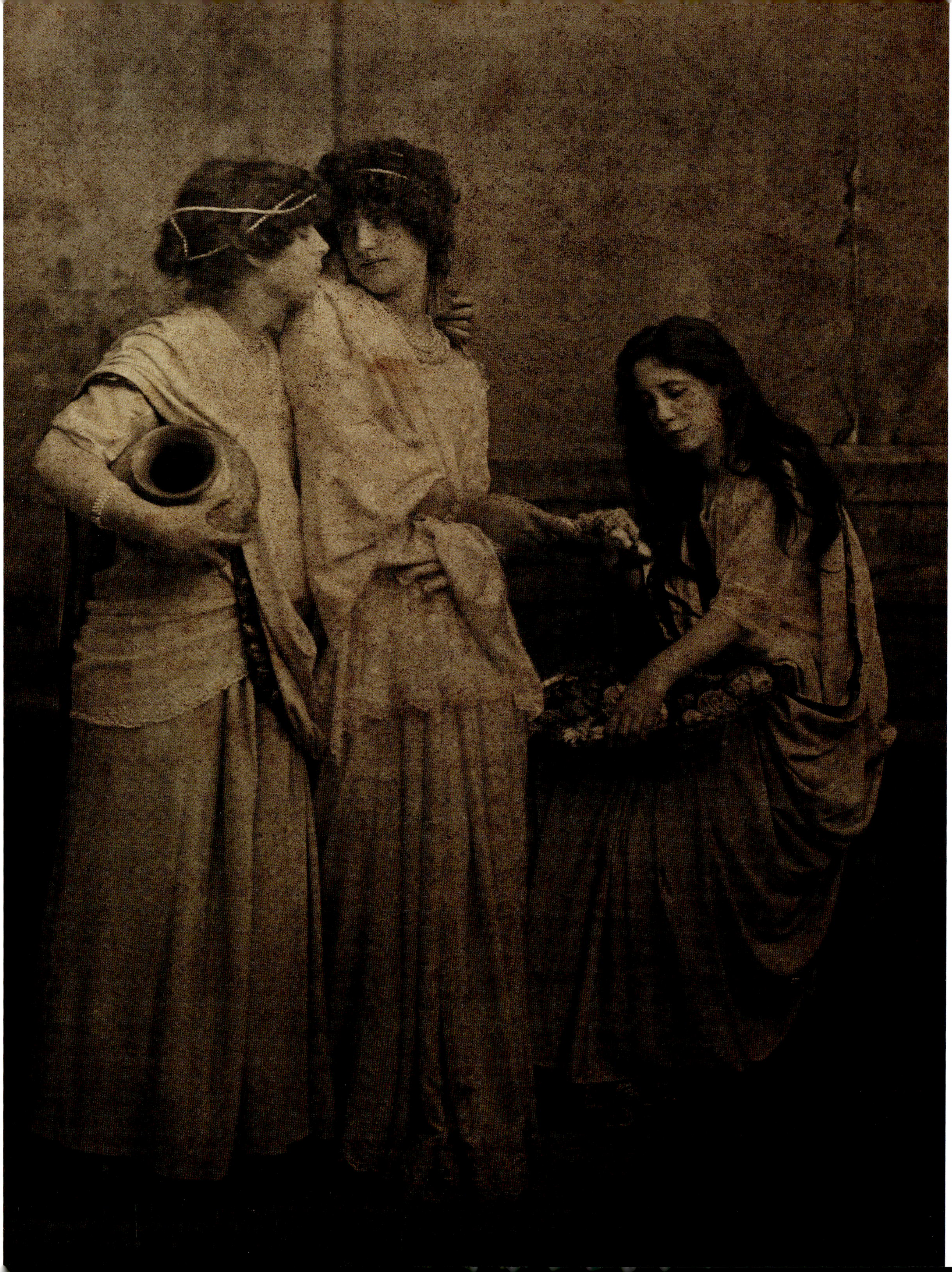

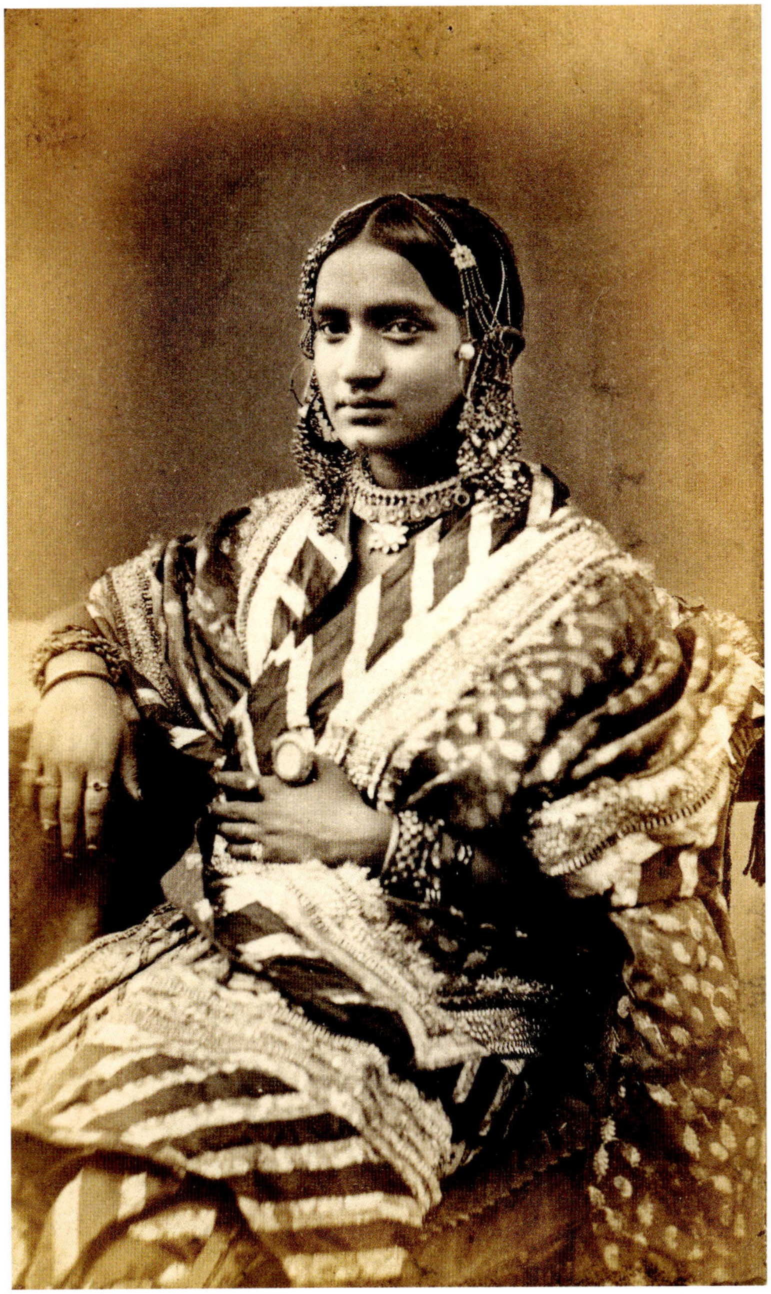

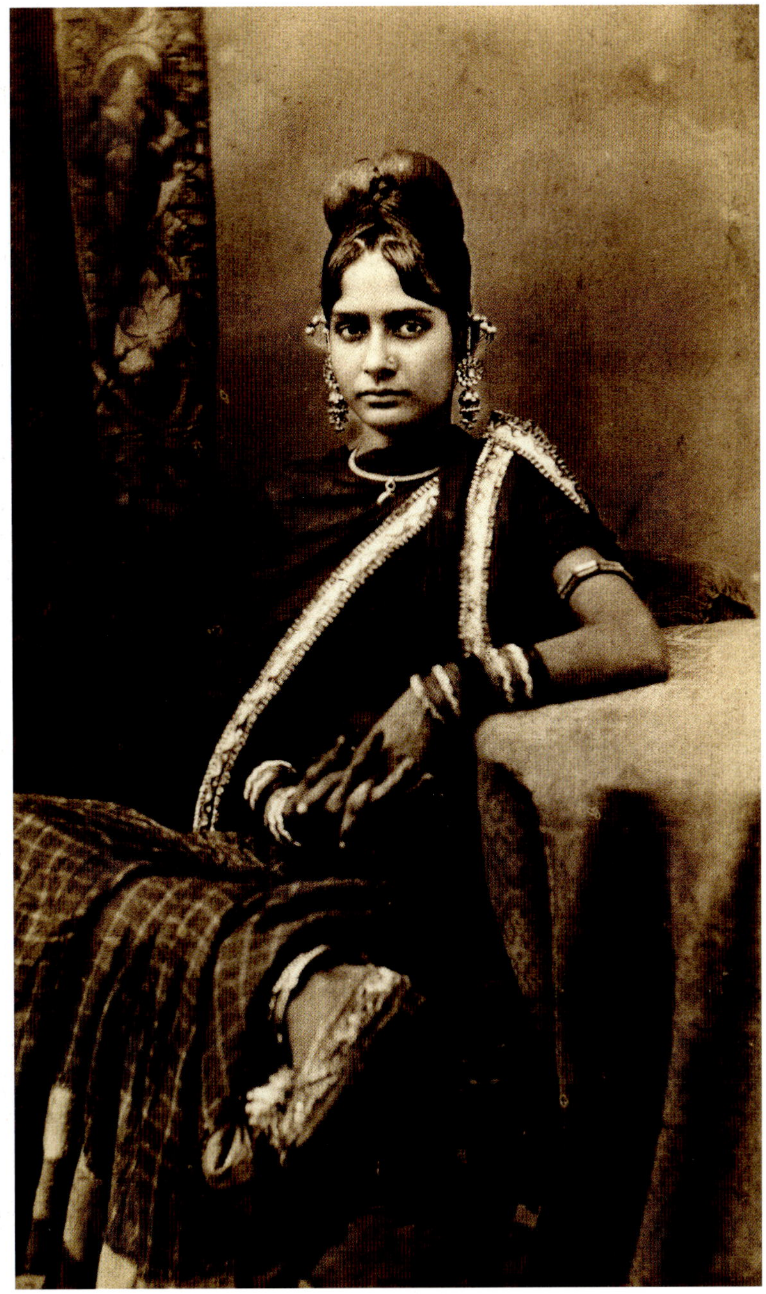

FIG. 4(A–B) | DAROGHA ABBAS ALI
*Seated Lady of the Court (a) & (b)*
albumen carte-de-visite, 104 x 62 mm, c. 1870s
[ACP: (a) 98.64.0011; (b) 98.64.0012]

FACING PAGE
FIG. 3 | SHAPOOR N. BHEDWAR
*The Feast of Roses—The Flower Girl*
carbon print, 349 x 261 mm, c. 1890s,
from the *Art Studies* album [ACP: 97.47.0001 (06)]

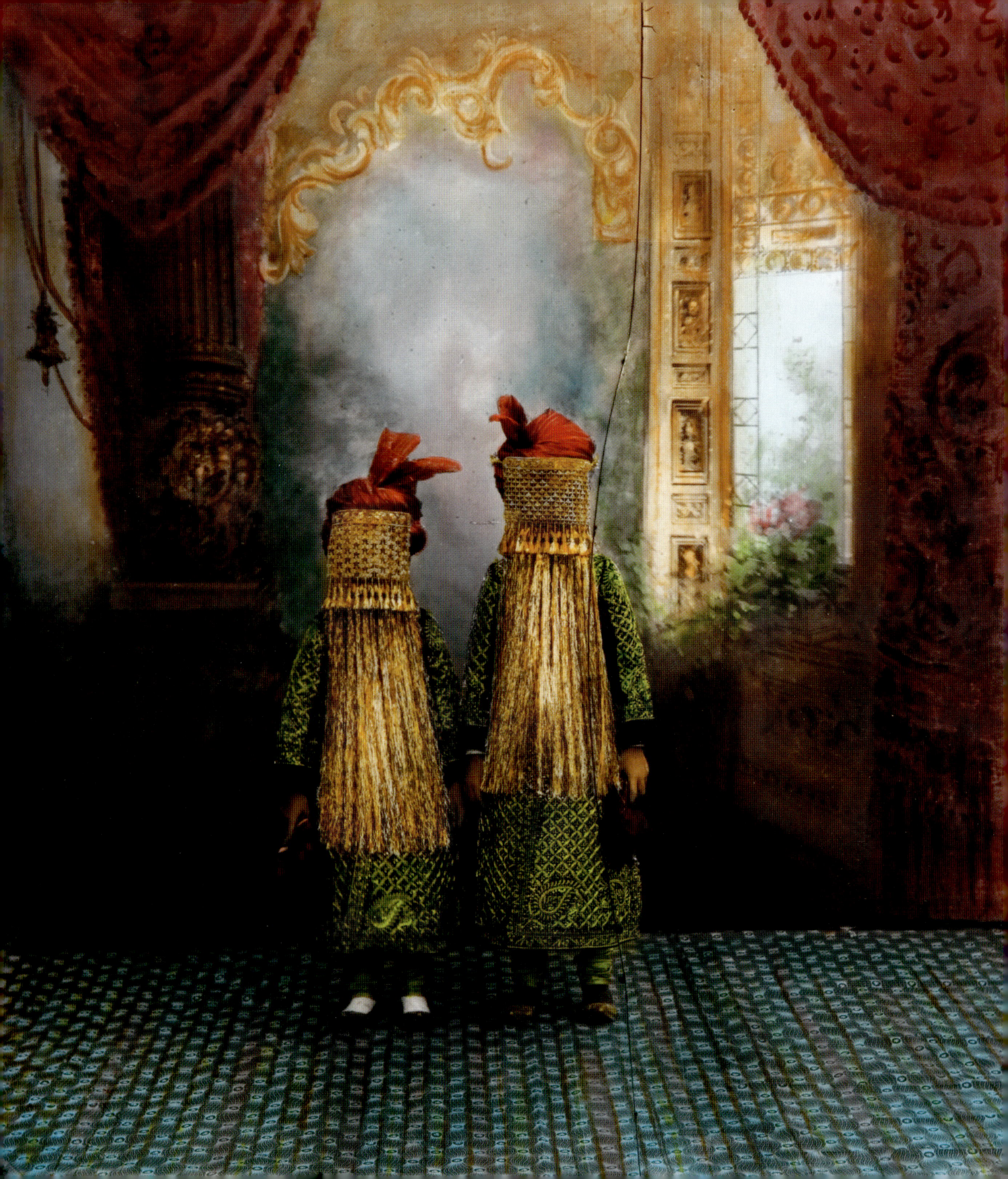

Ali may have found a lucrative subject in these nautch girls, a subject that also captured the imagination of several European artists in India in subsequent years.

The development of the studio portrait gave the middle classes access to a genre that had hitherto been confined to oil portraits of the nobility. Among these early group photos, I have chosen two striking portraits: one of them from none other than the princely family of Bhopal, the grandsons of Begum Sultan Shah Jahan dressed up for a wedding (Fig. 5), and the other an earlier image of the Begum herself (Fig. 6). The portrait of the two veiled princes seem to subvert the prime function of portraiture, that is, to capture the facial likeness of the sitter. On the other hand, the dramatic image of the Begum herself informs us about how the custom of *purdah* was not strictly followed even when the ruler was a female. As a ruler, considered divine by her subjects, she was exempt from the usual constraints faced by women. In this she was no different from princely men who, as we know from innumerable Mughal miniatures, were represented as divine.

## The Mughal Legacy in Indian Photography

To return to the Mughal legacy in photography, I try and offer here a bare outline of its myriad implications for the colonial era. In the process, I hope to throw some light on the and contradictory pulls between the "modern" British Empire, and the pre-modern Mughal civilisation, which the colonial rulers overturned. An interesting aspect of this is the political manipulation of the Mughal legacy. Renouncing the idea that Western reforms could improve Indian society, after 1857, British rule was predicated on the image of a timeless India that was inimical to Western progress.[9]

Modern nations often take recourse to the old tradition in order to assert a mythical continuity with the historic past. The late Barnard Cohn showed us how the Raj "re-invented" Mughal rituals in order to legitimate British authority over Indians. In the post-1857 era, the official tour was incorporated into the Mughal concept of the Durbar.[10] Originally, the Durbar was the meeting of the Mughal emperor with the nobles of the realm. Emperor Shah Jahan had choreographed a formal hierarchy of the nobles of the reign, with himself at the apex.[11] The English did not employ the Mughal pyramid—they created a different kind of hierarchy with the viceroy as the figurehead. The two most sumptuous durbars were the great Durbar of Delhi held by Lord Curzon in 1903, followed in 1911 by the Durbar of King George V, the only reigning monarch to visit India. These durbars were meant to demonstrate that the Indian princes under their British colonial overlord were more representative of the Indian sentiment than the minority of Western-educated nationalists (Fig. 7).

The man who captured the pomp and circumstance of the British Raj was Lala Deen Dayal, the leading Indian photographer of the Victorian Age, who was appointed photographer to Queen Empress herself. Many of these grand assemblages and other forms of imperial "theatre"

FIG. 5 | UKNOWN PHOTOGRAPHER; UNKNOWN ARTIST
*Grandsons of Begum Sultan Jahan of Bhopal: Habibullah Khan (1903–1930) & Wahid uz-Zafar (1905–1922)*
gelatin silver print and watercolour, 297 x 250 mm, c. 1910s [ACP: D2004.119.0001]

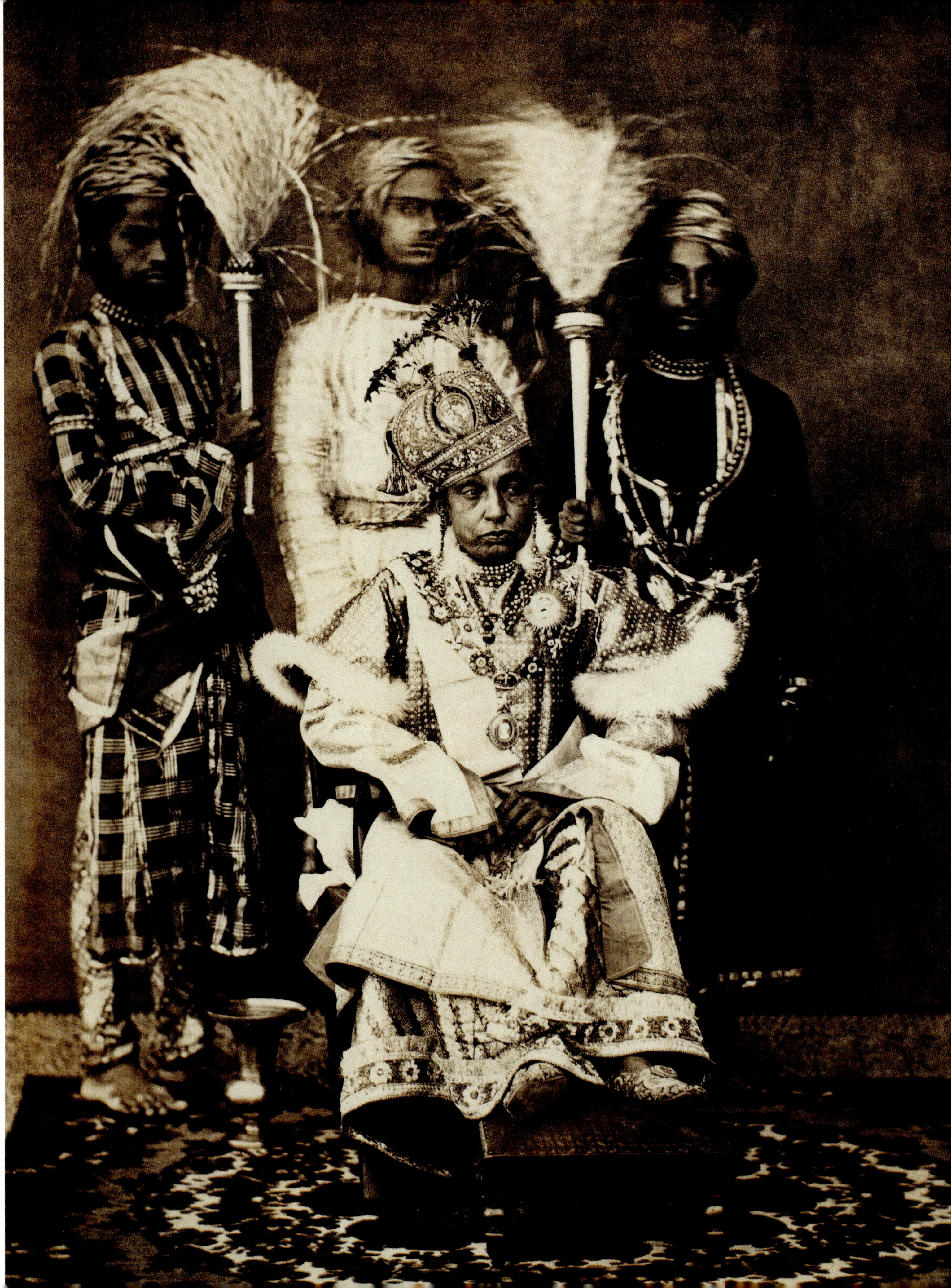

were recorded by a plethora of photographers but few left as great a mark as Deen Dayal. He stood at a vantage point to witness and represent the imperial spectacle. A man of unusual talent and organising ability, Deen Dayal established large photographic studios in several cities, including Bombay, employing assistants, as well as opening a special section of women assistants who were allowed access to the women's quarters of respectable households. His brilliant images based on large glass negatives often employed long shots and deep diagonals that dramatically enhanced the panoramic view of a scene. This is seen, for instance, in his pictures of the colonial armed forces; and even in official group portraits, he avoided a conventional frontal pose in favour of a diagonal view to considerable effect.[12]

## Camera and the Indian Eye

Did the practice of photography in India give rise to a unique visual language that singled them out in the global history of photography? The faith of the British Raj in the camera as the machine that eliminated all subjective bias in order to capture the truth was part of the nineteenth-century romance of scientific objectivity. People were impressed because of the "real presence" in a photograph. Yet the old adage "the camera does not lie" was debunked long ago. Judith Mara Gutman produced a major work arguing that photography by Indians, especially popular tinted photographs, represented the Indian perception of reality. In combating Western prejudice and neglect of Indian photographers, did she fall into the trap of proposing an "essentialising" contrast between India and the West?[13]

It is not so much a special Indian perception of reality, I would argue, as the particular visual conventions or pictorial language that invested Indian photography with a singular quality.[14] These visual conventions themselves became more complicated in the colonial period. Therefore in order to understand the actual impact of photography in India, we need to widen our scope to probe the general role of Western naturalist art in the whole field of colonial visual culture. Simply put, photography had a very different impact in India from that in the West. Photography, it has been remarked, was the logical culmination of the Western quest for mimesis in visual representation. It also fulfilled another peculiarly Western preoccupation: the search for the perfect replica where you cannot tell the difference between the original and its reproduction. A long historical process in the West led to a series of inventions, including lithography in the nineteenth century. It was in order to convey the peculiar qualities of light and shadow as well as the texture of reality in painting that pioneers like Fox Talbot and Daguerre stumbled upon photography—which is literally "drawing with light". The superior "truth value" of the camera made *trompe l'oeil* in painting redundant. Soon the avant-garde was forced to part company with mimesis.[15]

In India, colonial rule coincided with one of the great transformations of visual culture that broke away from earlier pictorial conventions, not least Mughal pictorial conventions.

FIG. 6 | JAMES WATERHOUSE
*Her Highness the Nawab Secunder, K.S.I., Begum of Bhopal*
albumen silver print, 163 x 110 mm, November 1862
[ACP: 98.72.0002.1 (71)]

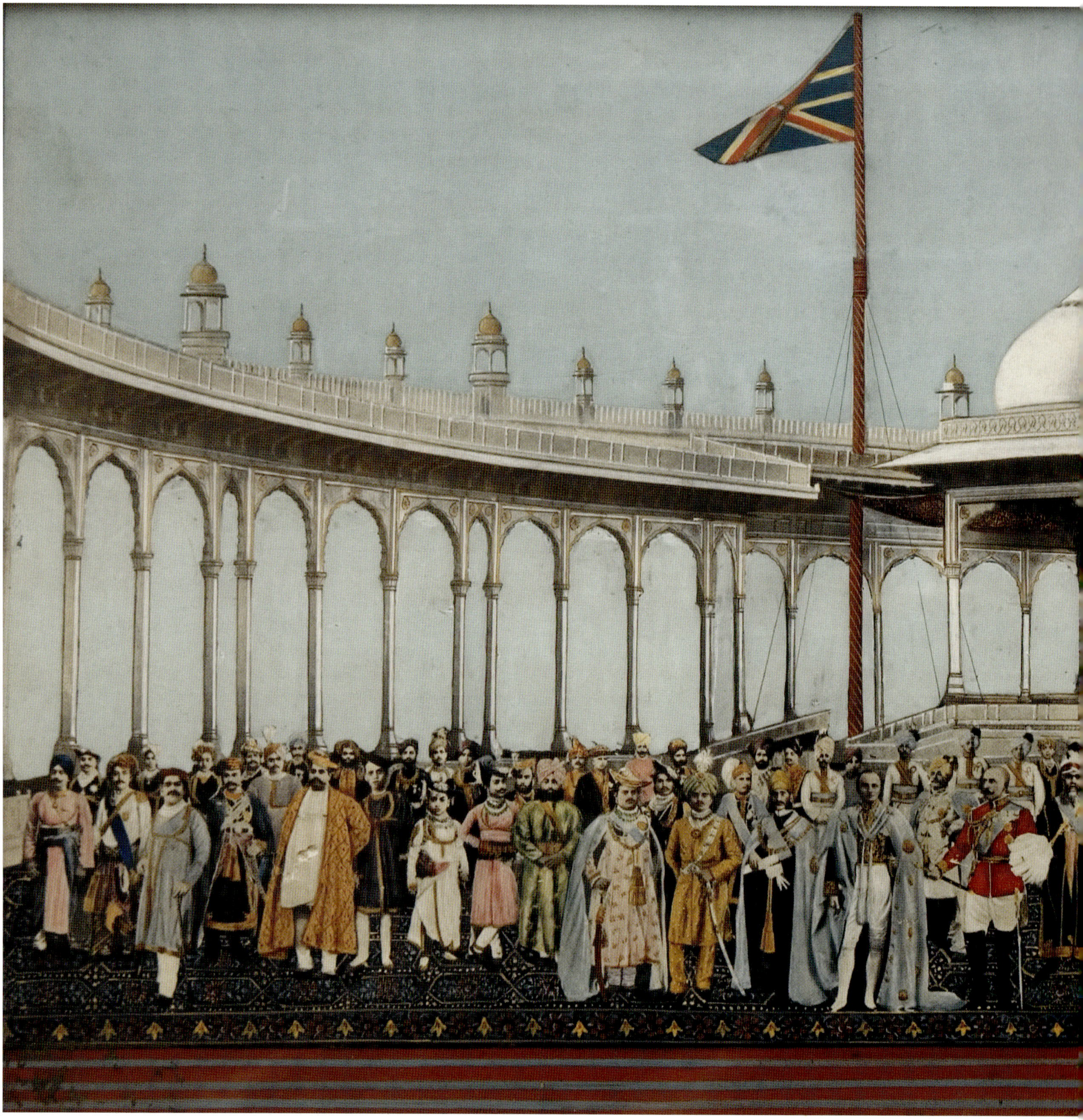

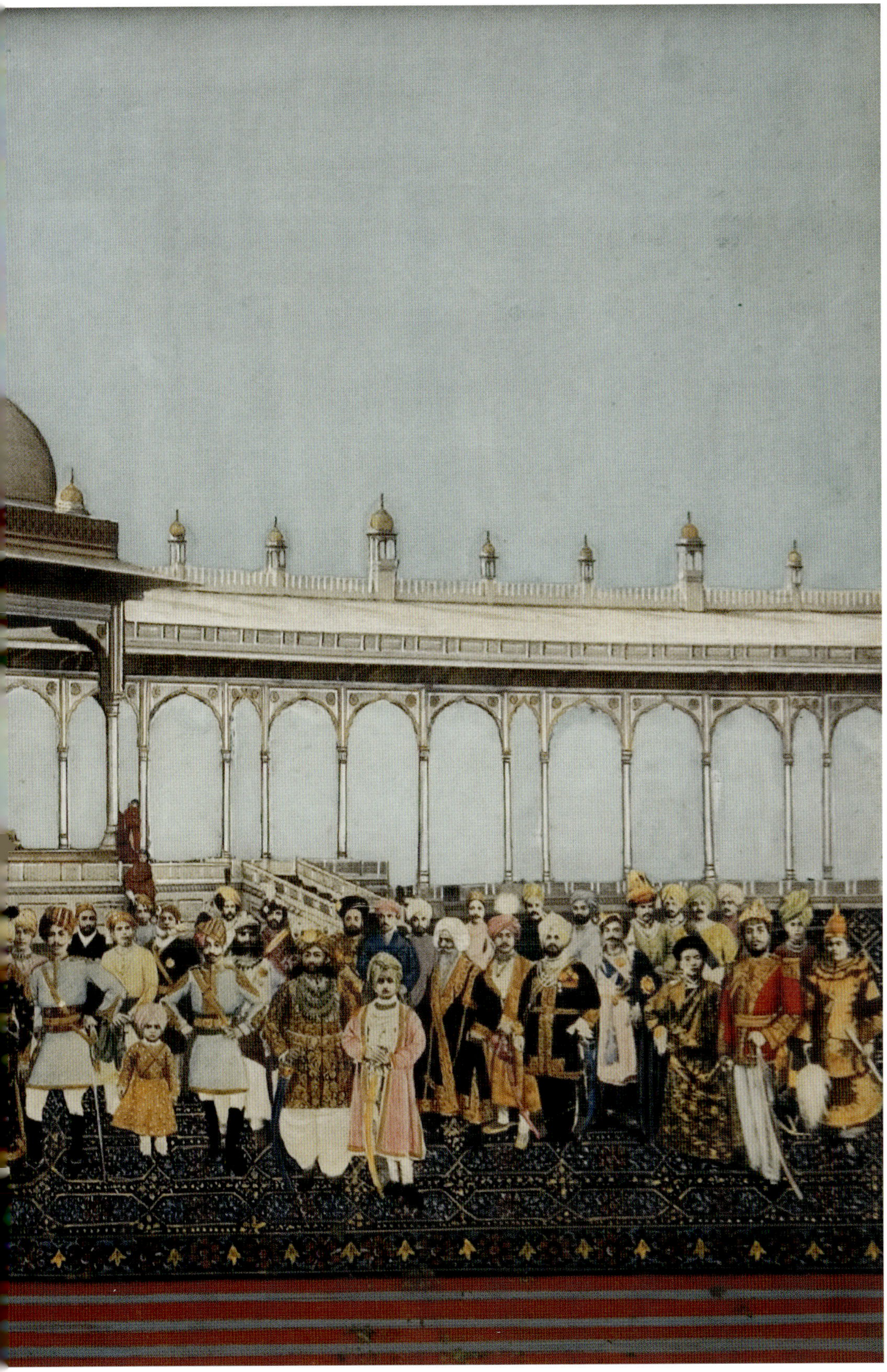

FIG. 7 | VERNON & CO., BOMBAY; UNKNOWN ARTIST
*Imaginary Scene of Lord Curzon and the Duke of Connaught Surrounded by Chiefs and Nobles of the Anglo-Indian Empire on the occasion of the Durbar of 1903*
hand-coloured gelatin silver print with gouache, 223 x 368 mm, c. 1903–1904 [ACP: 2005.05.0126]

Three related media, central to the rise of modernity in India, brought this about: Victorian academic painting; the processes of mechanical reproduction; and finally the camera. All these three made sustained assaults on the Indian sensibility, which turned India into an "iconic culture". This interrelationship between the three visual media made India's response to photography very different from that in the West.[16]

In short, Victorian illusionist painting became the hallmark of colonial India. Its celebrated exponent was the aristocratic Raja Ravi Varma (1848–1906). He laid down the benchmark for naturalism, with his portraits eagerly commissioned by notables ranging from British dignitaries to the Indian aristocracy. Varma's imaging of the Indian past inspired early nationalists while his oleographs entranced unlettered millions. There is a fascinating episode, which brought Ravi Varma the most important painter, and Deen Dayal the most important photographer, of nineteenth-century India together. Elsewhere I have shown the importance of photographs as a source for the colonial artist including Ravi Varma. Conversely, the Indian photographer's debt to painting can be seen in an anonymous late-nineteenth century carte-de-visite, which is a clear homage to the magnificent oil portrait by Hansaji Raghunath of the Maharani of Baroda.

Christopher Pinney quotes Roland Barthes to make a pithy point:

> "even when ... the picture is entirely delivered over to the automatism of the camera, the taking of pictures is still a choice involving aesthetic and ethical values."[17]

As Pinney further suggests, Indian photographers actively sought to construct their Indian visual identities during British rule. While agreeing with this reasonable view, I would turn to an authority to make a slightly different point: Ernst Gombrich made us aware that as human beings we do not perceive things differently across cultures; it is simply that our artistic conventions determine our representation of the visible reality.[18] It is not so much the particular Indian vision, since our perception as human beings is governed by certain universal rules, as the culturally constructed artistic conventions that affected the Indian photographer, the accumulated armoury of technical and other cultural influences that he drew upon.

Mughal tendency towards naturalism was further strengthened with the discovery of European mimesis: chiaroscuro, single-point perspective and the preference for eye-level rather than the Persian aerial view. While the Mughal style spread over India, by the seventeenth century, provincial courts of Rajasthan and the Punjab began to enrich the Mughal tradition in the light of their cultural demands. Yet these paintings cannot be imagined without the previous Mughal developments. In portraits, the artists still aim for likeness, but subtle changes have taken place—colours are deeper and lines simpler, as lyricism replaces the clinical precision of Mughal high art.[19] The formal strength of pure lines and colours is stressed by making the figures flat, which are then set against a shallow, often flat neutral ground, something that the nineteenth-century

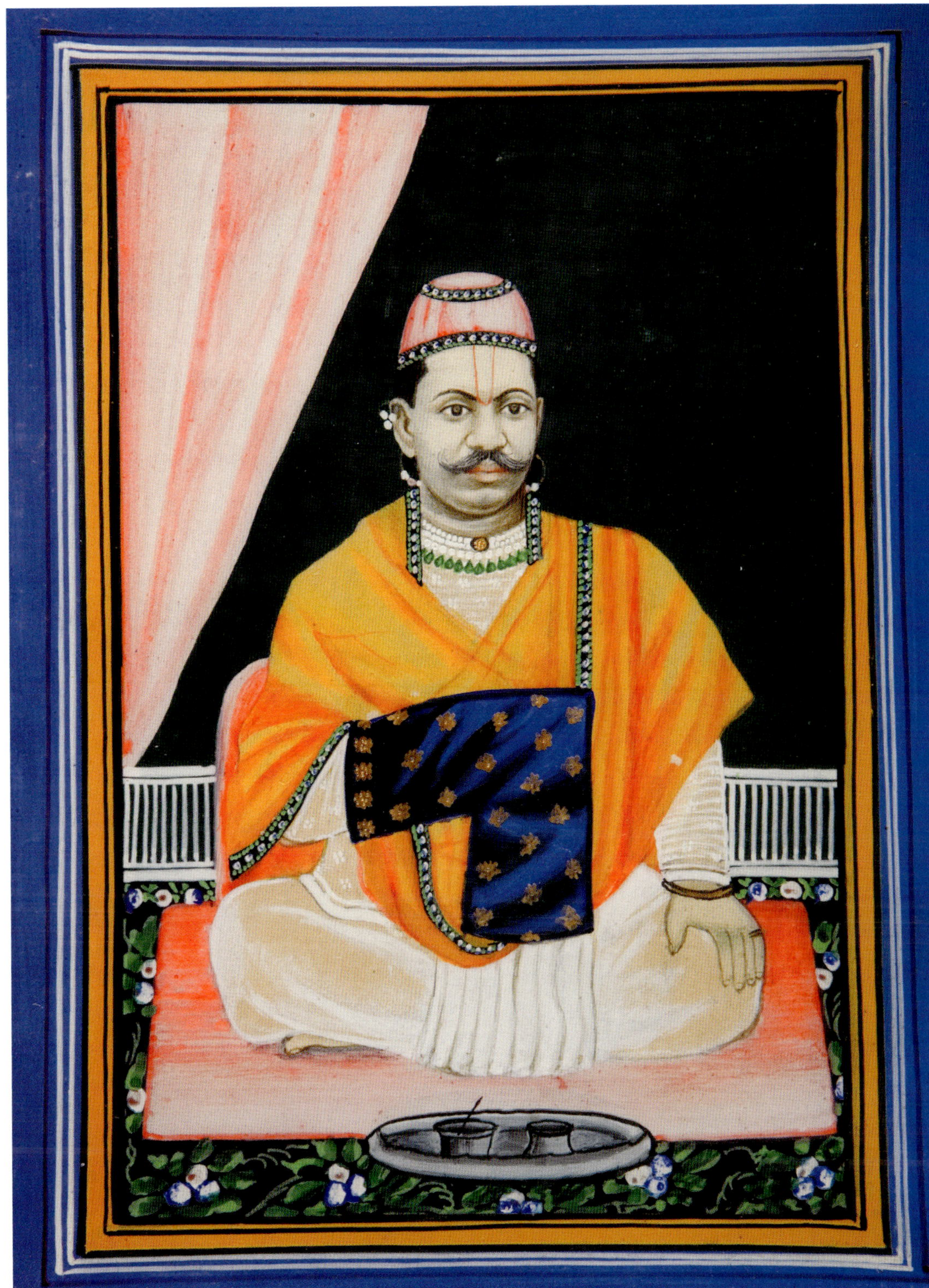

FIG. 8 | UNKNOWN PHOTOGRAPHER; ARTIST GHASIRAM HARDEV SHARMA (1868–1930)
*Swami Tilakayat Govardhanlalji (1862–1934) Head Priest of the Srinathaji Temple, Nathdwara*
gelatin silver print and watercolour, 168 x 123 mm, c. 1890s–1900s [ACP 98.83.0186]

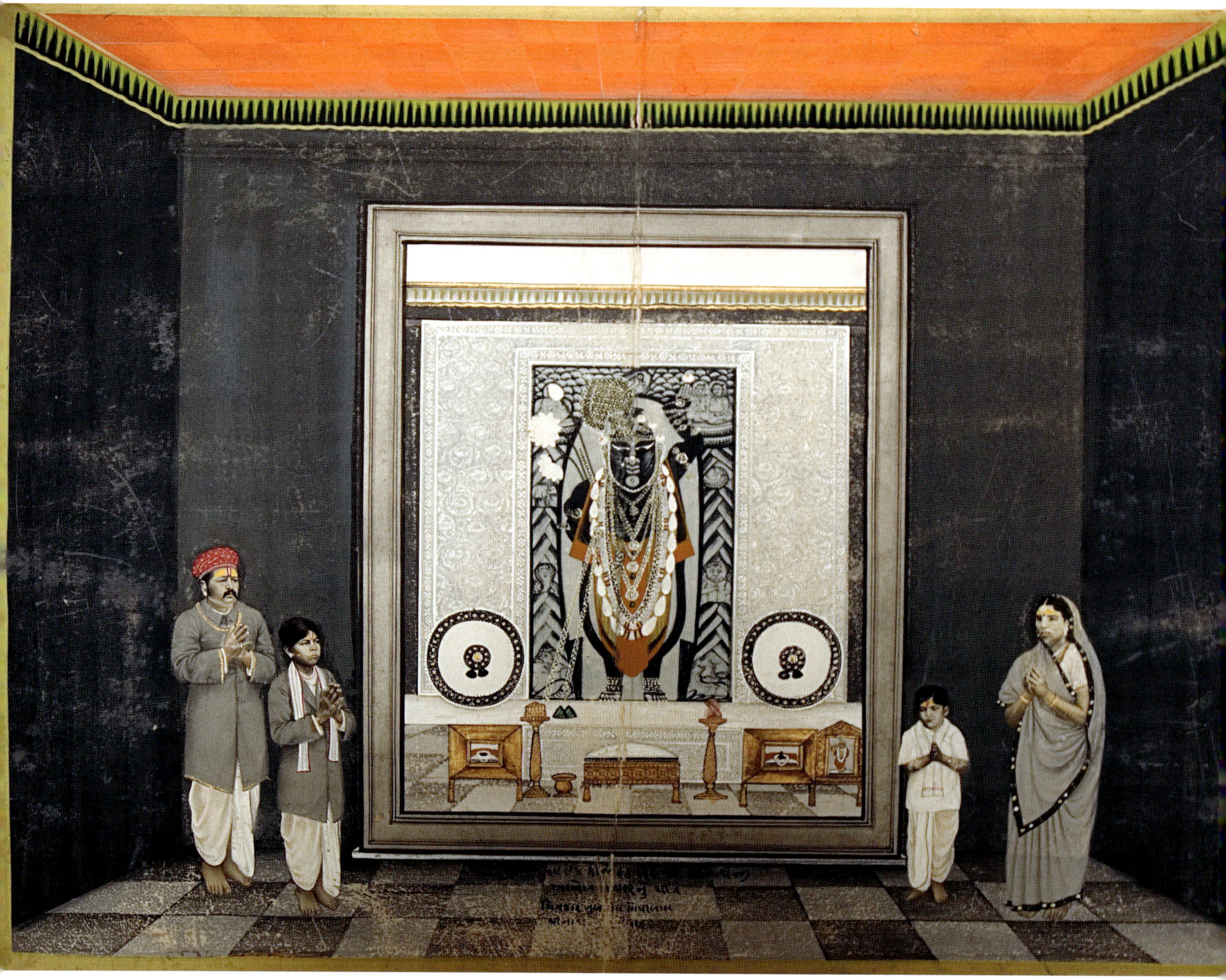

photographers were to exploit effectively (Fig. 8). I want to call the visual language that replaced the high Mughal aesthetic as post-Mughal, where earlier non-naturalist traditions of Rajasthan reassert themselves.

Of the confluence of three pictorial conventions in Mughal painting—pre-Mughal, Persian, and European—the pre-Mughal dominates the popular arts of colonial India. I am thinking of small-format, enclosed spaces with a tendency to flatten out the figure against a shallow ground, as well as bright, elementary colours and intricate decoration of the painted surface, in other words, the thriving trade in tinted or painted photographs. Admittedly, photographers in the West also tinted their pictures in response to demand. However, in India, there was a significant difference: an independent genre of painted photographs evolved in the subcontinent, which ranged from lightly tinted works to the slow transformation of photographs into paintings and finally into icons for worship. Even Ravi Varma emulated photographs, while photographers emulated compositions and figure arrangements of painted portraits.[20] What is relevant in this context is the tension between the universal aspects of the camera in its usage and technical possibilities, and the culturally specific pictorial conventions, a tension that brings us back to the post-Mughal legacy (Fig. 9).

Even though India was by no means the only country to introduce mass prints in popular religious art, mechanical reproductions, including the photograph, took on an independent life as sacred icons. With the introduction of the new mass media, printed images were transmuted into portable icons for household use. These prints thus lost what Walter Benjamin calls their modern "exhibitionary" value, as they acquired a new "cult value".[21]

To end these brief reflections on Indian photography, the mechanical device that appeared to replicate reality perfectly enthralled Indians as it fascinated people the world over. However, it is important to remember that this was only part of the Indian fascination with the whole world of Victorian illusionism, which was replicated endlessly in cheap oleographs or studio photographs (Fig. 10). Gradually the time-honoured conventions, which I have identified with the post-Mughal visual language, infiltrated the modernist utopia of perfect objectivity. And this subversion, I would suggest, is one of the lasting legacies of the Mughal civilisation that remained in collective memory, helping to create a specific pictorial language of Indian photography.

FIG. 9 | UNKNOWN PHOTOGRAPHER; UNKNOWN ARTIST
*Family Worshipping Shrinathji*
albumen silver print and watercolour
450 x 605 mm, c. 1900s [ACP: D2009.07.0006]

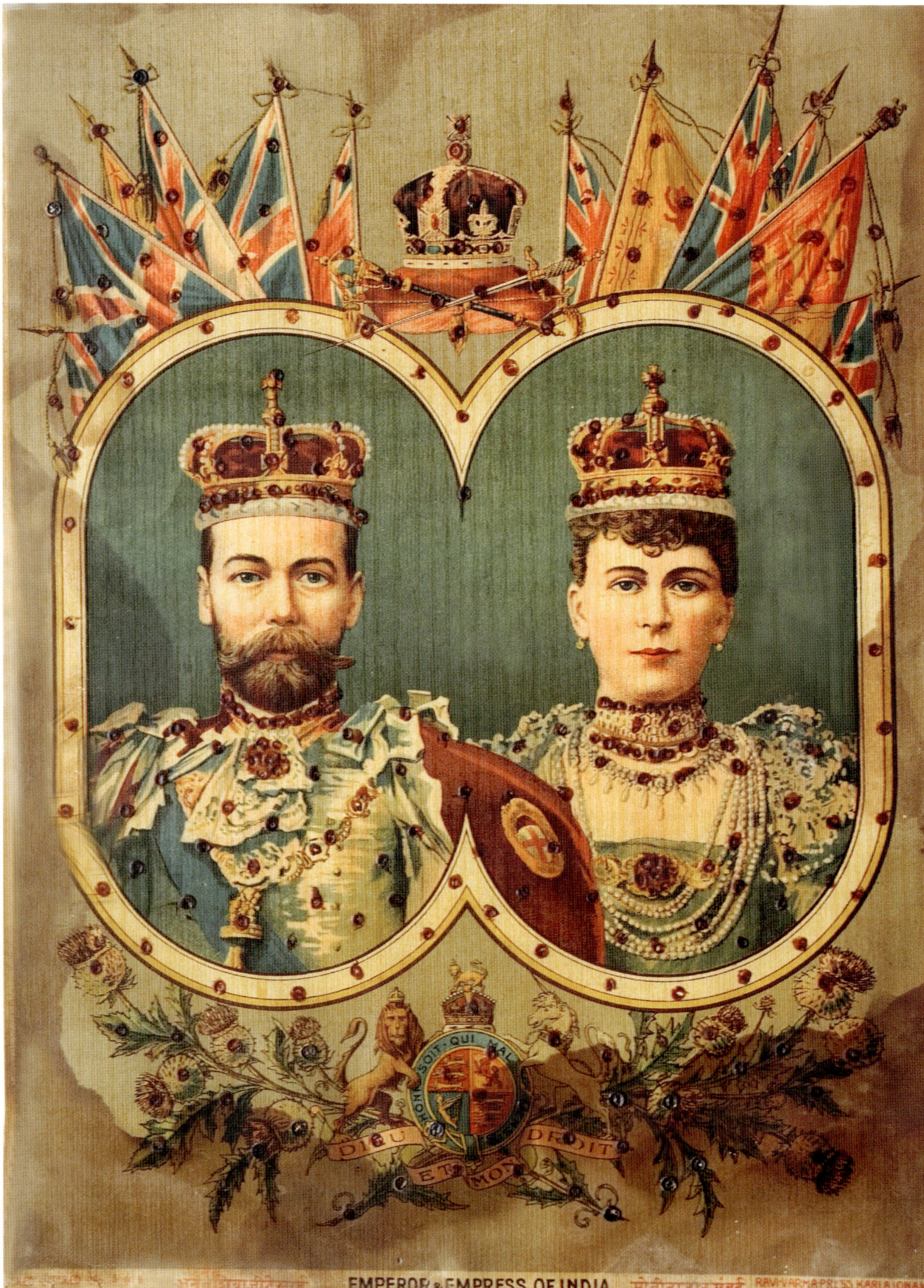
HONI SOIT QUI MAL
DIEU ET MON DROIT
EMPEROR & EMPRESS OF INDIA
मोतीबाजार मुंबई
RAVIVARMA PRESS KARLA LONAVLI

FIG. 10 | RAVI VARMA PRESS
*Emperor and Empress of India*
oleograph, 350 x 255 mm, c. 1900s
Registered 509, (Anantshivajidesai, Motibazaar, Mumbai)
[ACP: 98.83.0216]

NOTES

1 In 1982, I was invited by the Festival of India Committee of Britain to curate an historical exhibition entitled *Photography in India—1858–1980*, at the Photographers Gallery in London (Catalogue, *Photography in India—1858–1980*, London, 1982). I now return to the questions that I had originally posed in the essay that I wrote for the show. Due to space constraints I was unable to include the valuable notes and sources I had originally researched for the show. I gave a longer version of the essay as Benjamin Zucker Lecture at the Sackler Gallery, Harvard University in 2007 and later to the Alkazi Foundation Conference at the School of Oriental and African Studies in 2008.

2 See G.B. Kauver and G.C. Sorensen, eds. *The Victorian Mind* (London: Cassel in association with The Victorian Society, 1969).

3 C. Pinney, *Camera Indica: The Social Life of Indian Photographs* (London: Reaktion Books, 1997), 72.

4 *The Journal of the Photographic Society of Bengal* nos. 1–3 (1857).

5 R. Desmond, "19th Century Indian Photographers in India", *History of Photography* I, no. 4 (Oct 1977): 314.

6 On Robinson's comment on Bhedwar and other details about him, see the periodical, *Photographs of the Year*, 1891 and 1892. On Bhedwar's biography, see *The Photogram* II (1895), 252 ff.

7 P.C. Bunnell, "Pictorial Effect", in *The Art of Photography—1839–1989*, exhibition catalogue, ed. Mike Weaver (New Haven and London: Yale University Press, 1989), 156–7.

8 S. Gordon, "A City of Mourning: The Representations of Lucknow, India in Nineteenth-century Photography", in *History of Photography* XXX, no. 1 (Spring 2006): 80–91.

9 Metcalf, T.R. *An Imperial Vision: Indian Architecture and Britain's Raj* (London and Boston: Faber and Faber, 1989).

10 B.S. Cohn, "Representing Authority in Victorian India", in *The Invention of Tradition*, eds. E. Hobsbawm and T. Ranger (Cambridge: Cambridge University Press, 1983), 165–209.

11 Koch, E. "The Hierarchical Principle of Shah-Jahani Painting", in *King of the World: the Padshahnama*, catalogue, eds. M.C. Beach and E. Koch (Sackler Gallery: Azimuth Editions 1997), 130–143.

12 See Luther on Deen Dayal. Narendra Luther, *Raja Deen Dayal: Prince of Photographers* (Hyderabad: Creative Point, 2003).

13 J.M. Guttman, *Through Indian Eyes: 19th and 20th Century Photography from India* (New York: Oxford University Press, 1982).

14 E.H. Gombrich, *Art and Illusion* (London: Phaidon Press, 1962), 55–78, 246–278.

15 P. Galassi, *Before Photography*, exhibition catalogue (Museum of Modern Art, New York, March–July 1981).

16 P. Mitter, *Art and Nationalism in Colonial India 1850–1922*, part two (Cambridge: Cambridge University Press, 1994) on the great art revolution in India during the colonial period.

17 C. Pinney, *Camera Indica: The Social Life of Indian Photographs*, 11.

18 E.H. Gombrich, *Art and Illusion*.

19 M.C. Beach, *Mughal and Rajput Painting* (Cambridge: Cambridge University Press, 1992), for succinct account of Mughal and Rajasthani painting.

20 On Ravi Varma, see my *Art and Nationalism in Colonial India*, ch. 5.

21 W. Benjamin, "The Work of Art in the Age of Mechanical Reproduction", in *Illuminations* (London: Penguin Books, 1955), 219–253.

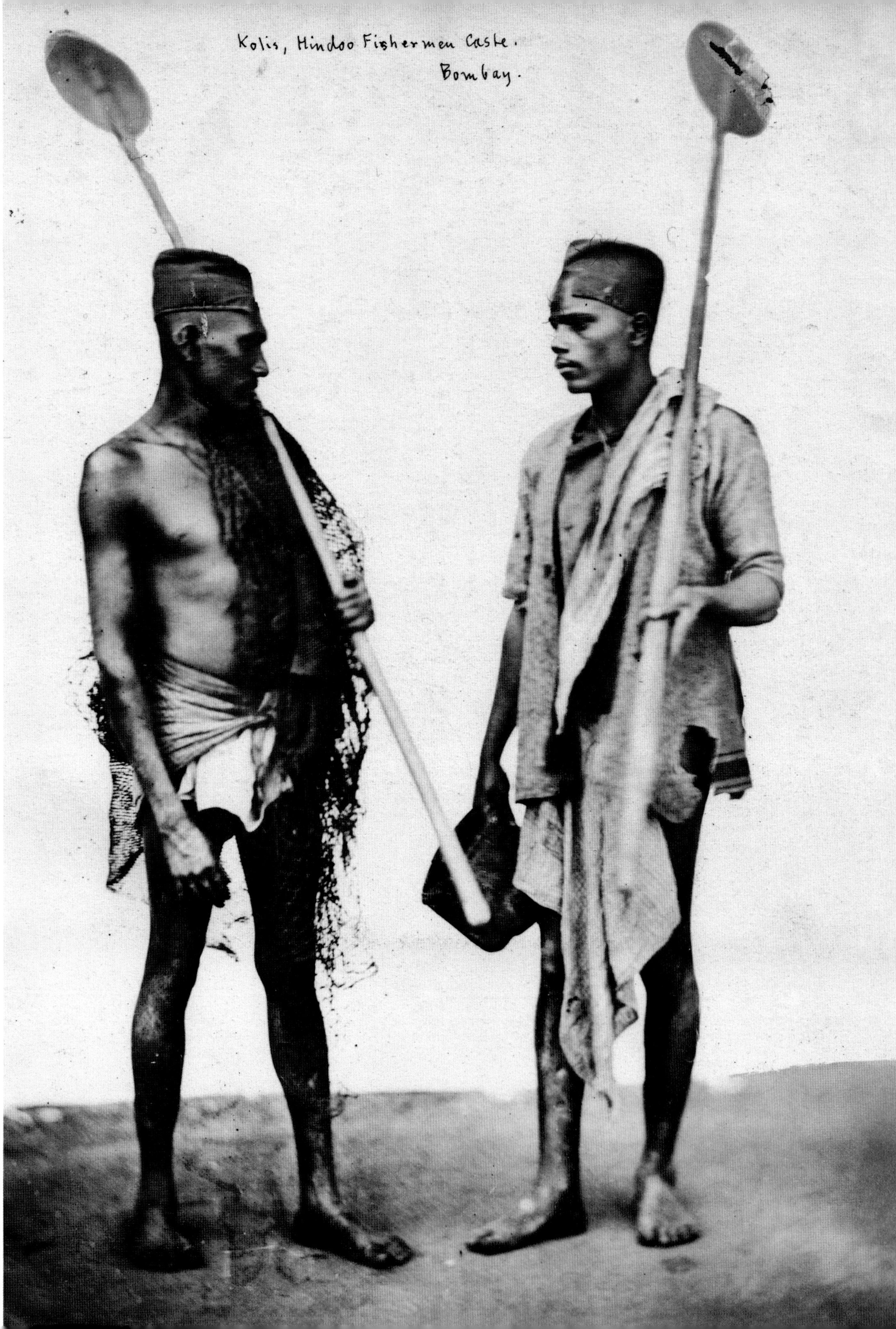
Kolis, Hindoo Fishermen Caste.
Bombay.

# Early Precedents
## Ethnographic Photography in Bombay, 1855–1870

Akshaya Tankha

*"Objects arise as figures in the landscape of empire; narratives and actions put them in motion"*
W.J.T. Mitchell in *What Do Pictures Want*[1]

### Introduction

Mitchell's telling remark on the nature of colonialism and collecting practices of that time finds an enchanting visual echo in the pages of photographic albums from the turn of the nineteenth century. Here we find several instances where the photographic image encompasses a journey as much as it does an illustration, reconfiguring objects as figures in the landscape of colonial photography.

When we take an image like Figure 11, shot against a uniformly covered backdrop, and juxtapose it with Figure 12, we see that the latter is subjected to a creative manipulation, in which the original photograph is reanimated as a composite print with an endless, montage landscape. Figure 11 appears unpolished, less than certain about how the people in the frame may be read. In comparison, the anonymous figures from the same community, fore-grounded against a faux depth of field in Figure 12, are now co-opted into the still emerging arena of ethnographic photography, coaxing the viewer to imbibe the visual association that the composite print enables between the sitters and the circumscribed world behind them. The concise caption and a lengthy descriptive account of the community in question, accompanying the image in Figure 12, may be read as the narrative that mobilizes these figures, putting them in motion within the realm of early anthropological photography—a genre actively nurtured under the gaze of the Raj.

While the particular subjects in the two images might have been different, the history of the two photographers and the lives of their images were intertwined in an intricate web of early photographic practice that flourished in Bombay [now Mumbai] in the 1860s. Brought together as part of this exhibition at the Dr. Bhau Daji Lad Museum, the vintage photographs showcase some of the earliest examples of ethnographic photography as practiced in India from the turn of the nineteenth century. Although somewhat nebulous as a genre, these early precedents are critically important to study the seeds of what became integral aspects of the field in later years. At the same time, it is pertinent to recognize the creative freedom that these pioneering experiments are characterized by, a freedom that gradually waned in the later repertoire of ethnographic imagery.

FIG. 11 | NARAYAN DAJI
*Kolis, Hindoo Fishermen Caste, Bombay*
albumen silver print, c. 1855–1870
[ACP: 2005.01.0001 (09)]

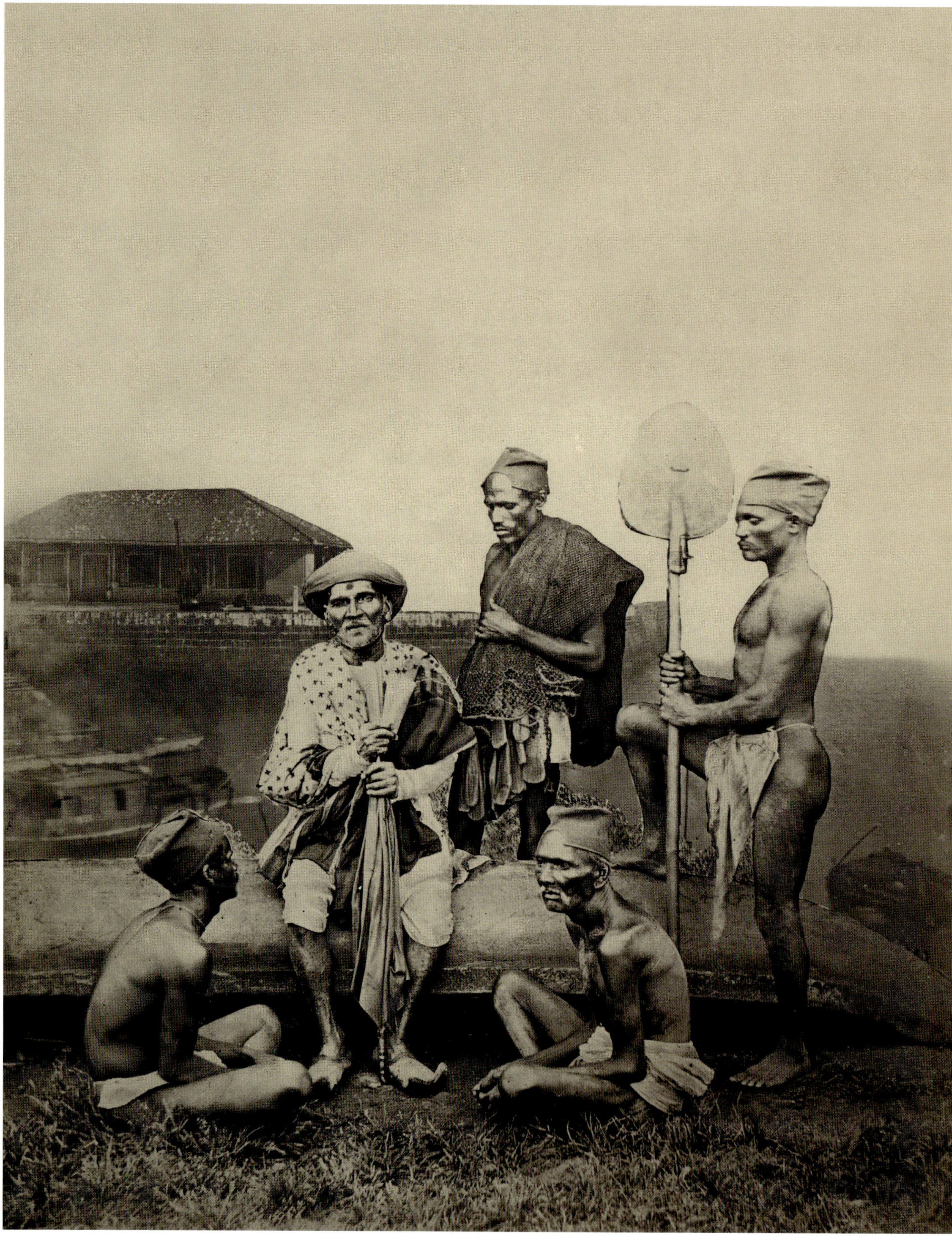

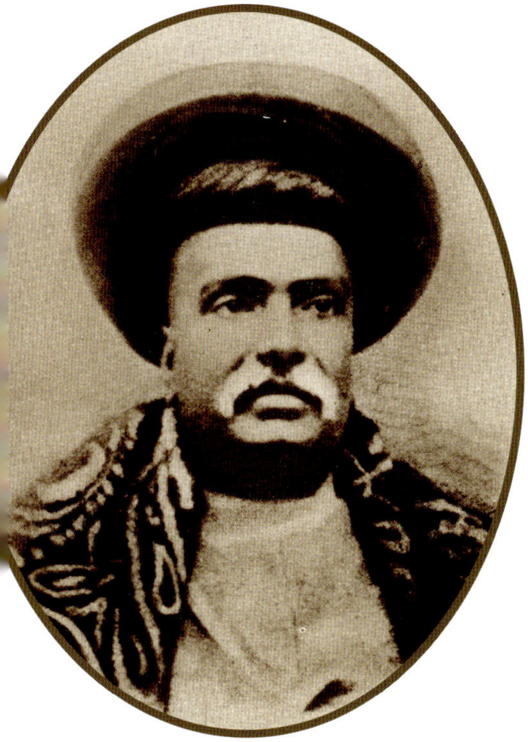

FIG. 13 | UNKNOWN PHOTOGRAPHER
*Dr. Narayan Daji*
Sourced from A.K. Priyolkar, *Doctor Bhau Daji: Vyakti, Kal v Kartutwa* (*The man, his age and his work*), 1971.

FACING PAGE
FIG. 12 | UNKNOWN PHOTOGRAPHER, POSSIBLY WILLIAM JOHNSON
*The Kulis of the West of India*
albumen silver print, 228 x 177 mm, c. 1866, from *The Oriental Races and Tribes, Residents and Visitors of Bombay* (Vol. II) [ACP: D2005.67.0001 (53)]

RIGHT
FIG. 14 | NARAYAN DAJI
*A Bhandaree or Toddeewalla, A Hindoo*
albumen silver print, 1855
[ACP: 2005.01.0001 (21)]

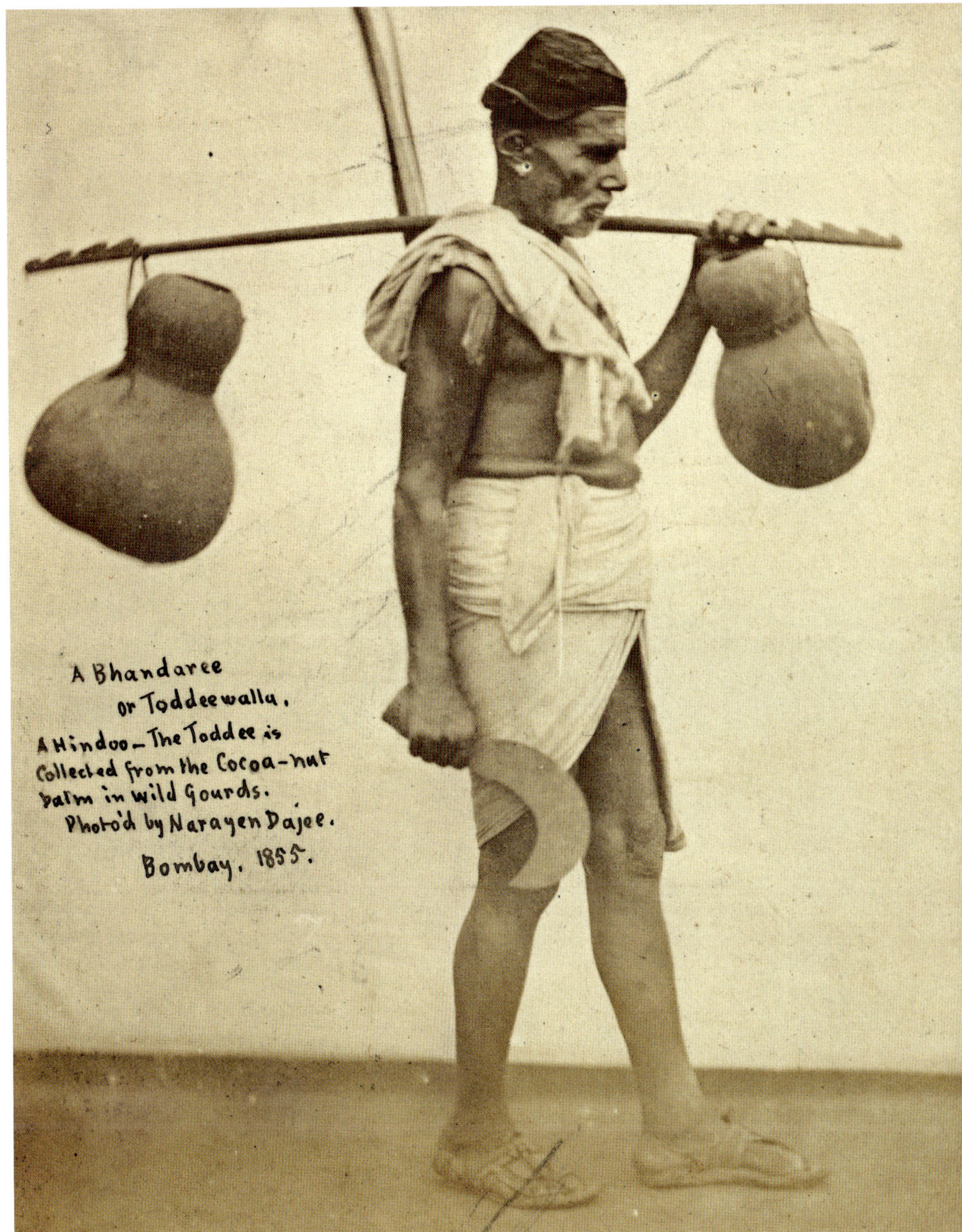

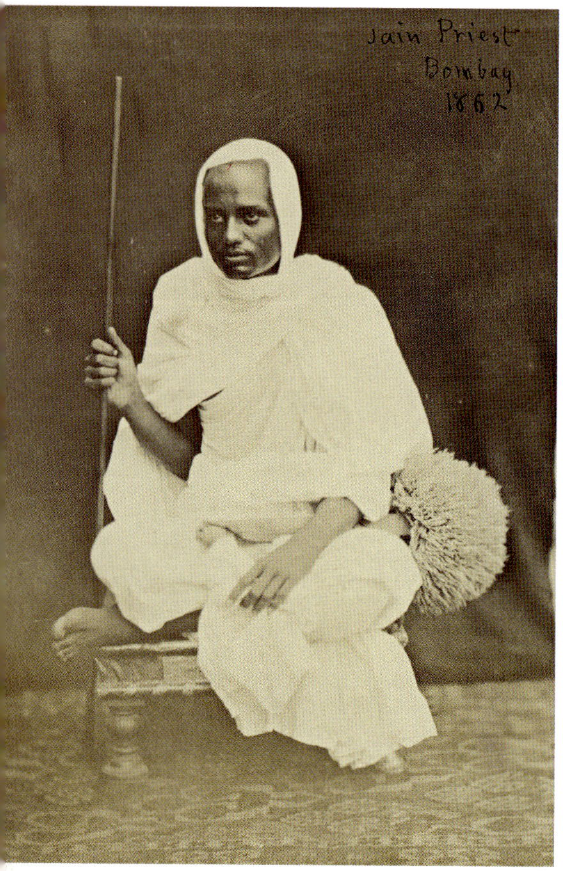


FIG. 15 | NARAYAN DAJI
*Jain Priest, Bombay*
albumen silver print, 1862
[ACP: 2005.01.0001 (20)]

FACING PAGE
FIG. 16 | NARAYAN DAJI
*Bhyrajeé, a worshipper of Ram-Chandra*
albumen silver print, c. 1855–1870s
[ACP: 2005.01.0001 (13)]

Both Narayan Daji (c. 1828–1875)[2] (Fig. 13)[3] and William Johnson were members of the Bombay Photographic Society, which was founded in 1854, two years before its counterparts came up in Calcutta and Madras [now Kolkata and Chennai respectively]. Supported by the commercial success and affluence of the port city, which enabled a healthy patronage of the novel photographic medium that was still out of reach for most, a number of studios emerged across the city, concentrated around Grant Road, Rampart Row and Kalbadevi Road among others. While Daji ran a studio on Rampart Row between 1858 and 1868, William Johnson reportedly worked out of Grant Road between 1855 and 1860.[4] Though their work as photographers was extensive, the present essay focuses on the corpus of their images that specifically relate to early ethnographic photography in India, a field that created an interesting dialogue between their efforts behind the lens and the broader narratives the images nourished: a gradually emerging knowledge-based Empire, the demands of state surveillance and a burgeoning public sphere that consumed and patronized photography.

## Narayan Daji

The first image (Fig. 11) belongs to the repertoire of Narayan Daji, one of India's earliest photographic practitioners. Along with his brother Dr. Bhau Daji Lad, after whom the museum was renamed [from Victoria & Albert Museum], Narayan Daji was among the earliest council members of the Bombay Photographic Society. His expertise with the medium was rare for the time, comparable with European exponents like Linnaeus Tripe and Thomas Biggs. He had even applied, albeit unsuccessfully, for the post of Instructor in Photography at Bombay's Elphinstone Institute in 1855.[5]

Narayan Daji's ethnographic oeuvre goes back to almost the same period. His was the largest selection of ethnographic portraits—31 in all—exhibited in Bengal Photographic Society's exhibition of 1857.[6] The portraits evoked a strong desire on the part of the exhibition's organisers to emphasise the need for undertaking further such photographic endeavours that were aimed at documenting the "castes and costumes" of the "natives".

European interests in ethnographic photography was geared largely towards a reification of visual markers for race in the colonies, and practiced simultaneously in Asia, Africa, Australia and the Polynesian Islands among other sites. Photographs such as Figure 14, of the Toddywala, highlight this association clearly. The caption, inked on the printed albumen paper, establishes a concrete relationship between the subject and his presumed identity—a designation transferred through the overlapping and confused affiliations of race, caste and occupation. Tools and implements used by subjects were also utilized, as in this case, to enact their role in society, within the circumscribed visual frame.

The precedents that paved the way for such practices of colonial collecting stemmed from an emerging interest in the arts and crafts of European colonies in Asia and Africa, which were

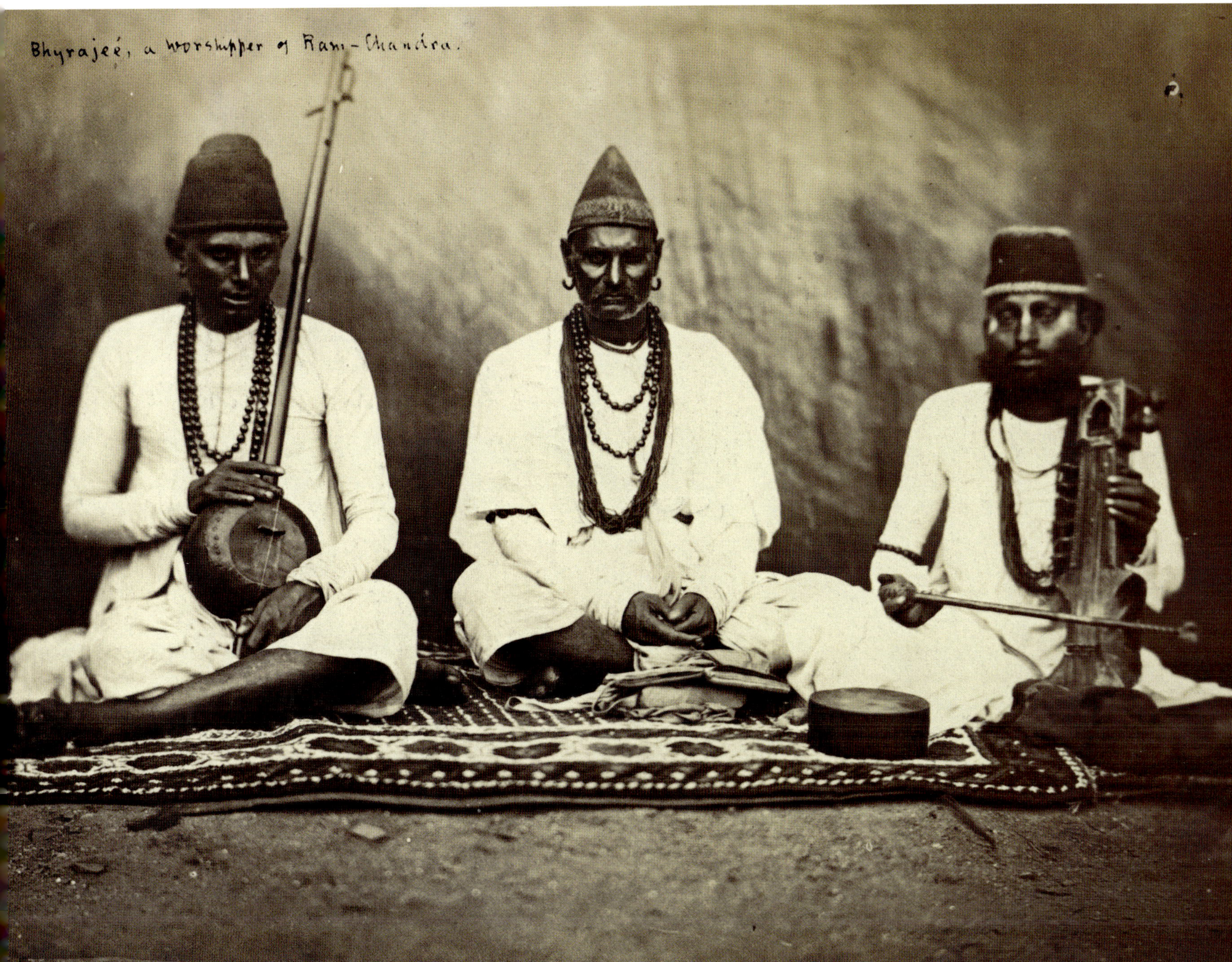
Bhyrajeé, a worshipper of Ram-Chandra.

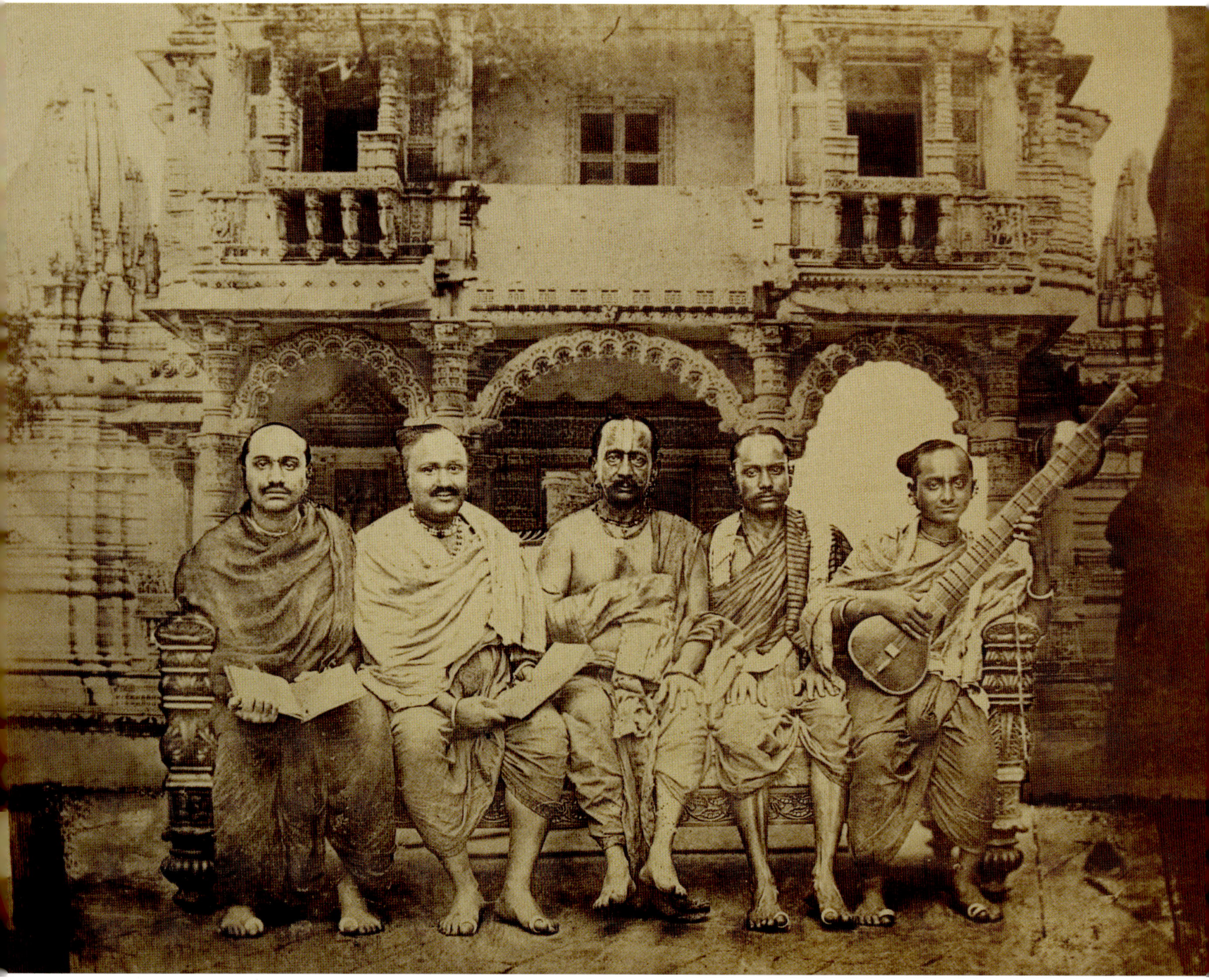

displayed alongside examples of industrial progress at international exhibitions, starting from the Great Exhibition of 1851 at Crystal Palace, London. "Specimens" of peoples were an associated object of fascination for the Orientalist collector. The novel technology of the camera came to be viewed as the perfect, objective medium by which the colonized racial "types" could be grasped and their variety ordered. Photographs were used to imagine people within a restricted frame of reference and as tangible information to create organized classifications, in the belief that these would be as stable as the chemicals that bound their image on the photographic surface.

While depictions such as the aforementioned figures seemed to adhere to the norms of this as-yet inchoate field of anthropological photography, there were other images such as Figures 15 and 16 that seemed to move away from this emphasis. Narayan Daji's focus in *Jain Priest* and *Bhairajees* moves away from an exclusively European, colonial interest in tracing the physical coordinates of the "native", and reflects a locally influenced, vernacular interest in visualizing "divinity" and perhaps even anticipating the idea of the mobile, personalized form of worship through its indexical capture, directed towards the viewer or devotee.[7]

Unlike the Koli fishermen against a bare background (Fig. 11) and the Toddywala (Fig. 14), the gaze of the Bhairajees (Fig. 16) who are highlighted as a community of worshippers, is directed towards the viewer. In this way, Narayan Daji's work seemed to adopt the aesthetic of ethnographic portraiture, using the same conventions for framing the priest and worshippers, yet widening its function from that of simply aesthetic and scientific contemplation to the possibility of reading the image as sacred and devotional.

This complex overlapping of scientific empiricism, anchored to the photograph as a verifiable document, and its possible religious efficacy, also comes through in *Vallabhacharya Maharajas* (Fig. 17), which was used in the first volume of *The Oriental Races and Tribes, Residents and Visitors of Bombay* edited by William Johnson. Photographed originally in the convention of Narayan Daji's earlier images, its reincarnation seen here as a composite image, replaces a plain cloth backdrop with a photographic image of a temple, thereby bringing forth the association between the sitters and their exalted, priestly identity. In later years, when photographs of high priests became popular as sacred imagery, the Vallabhacharya Maharajas were prominent among the communities that were willing subjects for photography, and their images circulated to pilgrimage centres such as Nathdwara.[8]

## William Johnson and *The Oriental Races and Tribes*

*The Oriental Races and Tribes, Residents and Visitors of Bombay* was one of the earliest ethnographic albums to be produced in the colonial world. Edited by William Johnson, a colleague of Narayan Daji and founder member of the Bombay Photographic Society,[9] two volumes were published, one in 1863 and the other in 1866, of the three that were to be originally produced.[10] Johnson was also a keen advocate of ethnographic portraiture, and had contributed images of

FIG. 17 | NARAYAN DAJI
***Vallabhachácháespecially Maharajas***

albumen silver print, 177 x 229 mm, c. 1863, from *The Oriental Races and Tribes, Residents and Visitors of Bombay* (Vol. I) [ACP: D2005.67.0001 (29)]

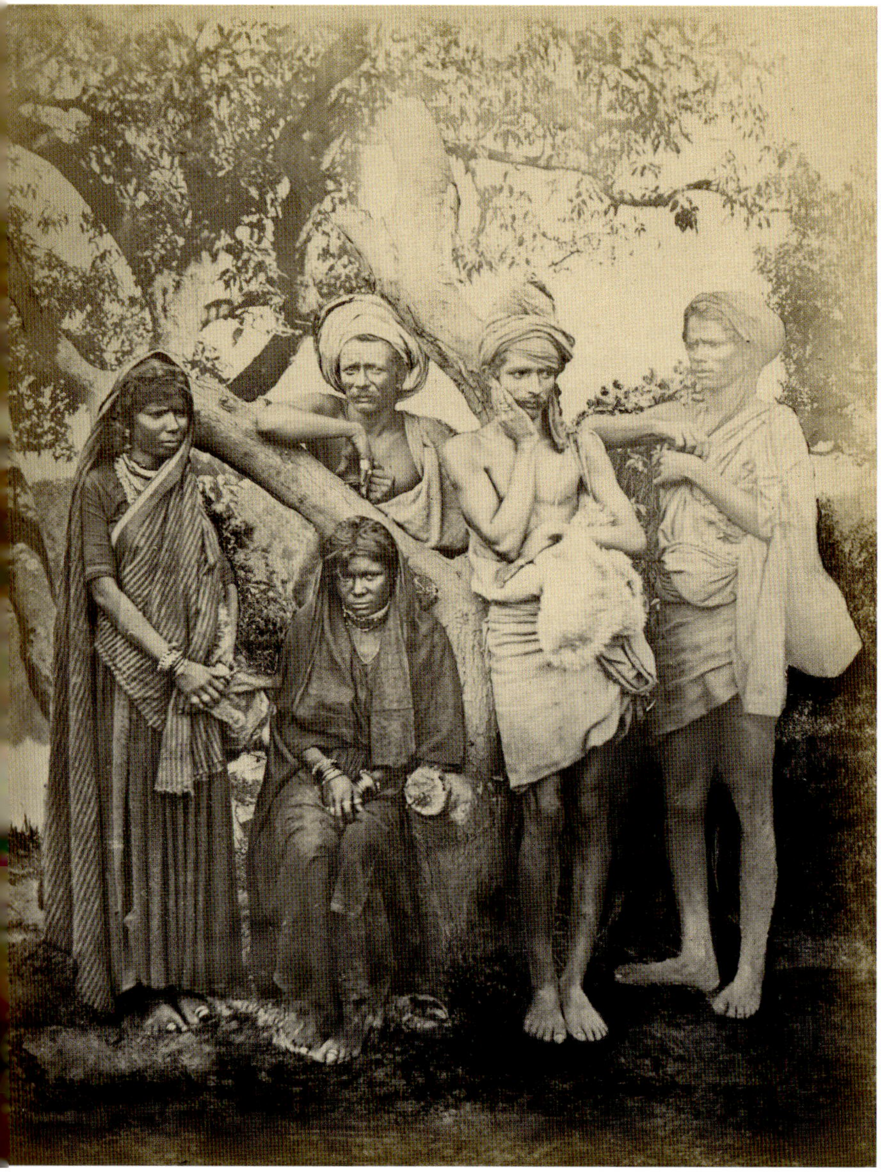

FIG. 18 | UNKNOWN PHOTOGRAPHER,
POSSIBLY WILLIAM JOHNSON
*Wâghurees*
albumen silver print, 230 x 176 mm, c. 1863,
from *The Oriental Races and Tribes, Residents and Visitors of Bombay* (Vol. I) [ACP: D2005.67.0001 (83)]

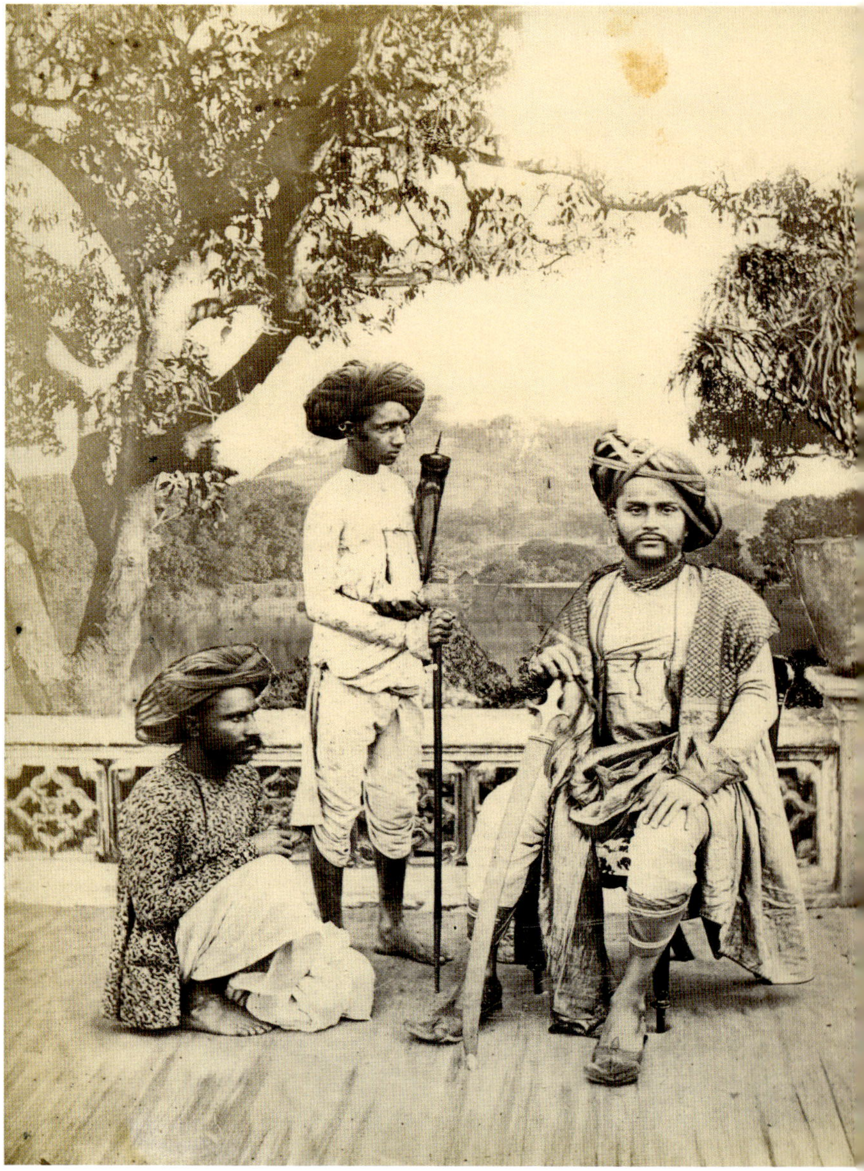

FIG. 19 | UNKNOWN PHOTOGRAPHER,
POSSIBLY WILLIAM JOHNSON
*Marathas of the Dakhan*
albumen silver print, 227 x 174 mm, c. 1863,
from *The Oriental Races and Tribes, Residents and Visitors of Bombay* (Vol. I) [ACP: D2005.67.0001 (99)]

"Costumes and Characters of Western India" for *Indian Amateurs Photographic Album*, which was produced in 24 parts between the years 1856 and 1858.[11] These photographs appear in *The Oriental Races and Tribes...* as montage images, set against photographic backdrops that range from the façade of a building, and a sweeping landscape, to a painted backdrop that one would have found in a conventional studio of the time.

Playfully created and widely circulated through its publication, what emerges in these albums is not only a host of composite montage images but an equally complex montage of "worldmaking",[12] bringing together a number of different, even contradictory, ways of representing the world that it purports to illustrate.

In Figure 18, sourced from the first published volume, the arrangement of people around a tree lends a degree of primitivity to the image of the Waghuree [Waghri] community, rendering them as bare and primeval, just as the forest that frames them. *The Kulis of Western India* follows a similar aesthetic mode of reckoning ethnic identity (Fig. 12), where the fishermen's tools of trade are held up as the primary markers of their existence. The barely-clad individual to the right, holding an oar, is made to stand in profile, a commonly used trope to "exhibit" physiognomy of the "racial type", supported by an elaborate textual description in the album that emphasizes the physicality of the oarsman.

These images together substantiate the introductory remarks by William Johnson in *The Oriental Races and Tribes...*, in which he states that the aim of the publications was to represent communities of India that converged in the Bombay Presidency, variously referencing "Darker Races" that are "exceedingly addicted to the worship of demons" and characterized as "Wild Tribes"; and listing the "Fairer races of the Hindus" while drawing affiliations with European nations, through linguistic similarities between Sanskrit and Latin[13] thus traversing racial and linguistic differences, to showcase the native "type".

However, the albums displayed far more than a conventional inventory of "types" commonly associated with nineteenth-century anthropological studies. Parsis, Bene Israelis and Roman Catholics along with smaller religious groups were also illustrated in this encyclopedic directory of communities in Bombay. The effort was thus towards assembling the widest possible selection of peoples across the communal spectrum. Much more than simply enumerating racial stereotypes, the textual narrative attempted to encompass references to social and cultural practices as well. Even pictorially, the montage images borrowed conventions of popular studio photography and popular theatre. Broadly stated, the albums were shaped by idiosyncrasies of photographers, designers and the publisher.

This comes forth in *Marathas of the Dakhan* (Fig. 19), in which the anonymity of the Kulis [Kolis] or Waghurees [Waghris] is contrasted with a personal reference to the seated person in the photograph:

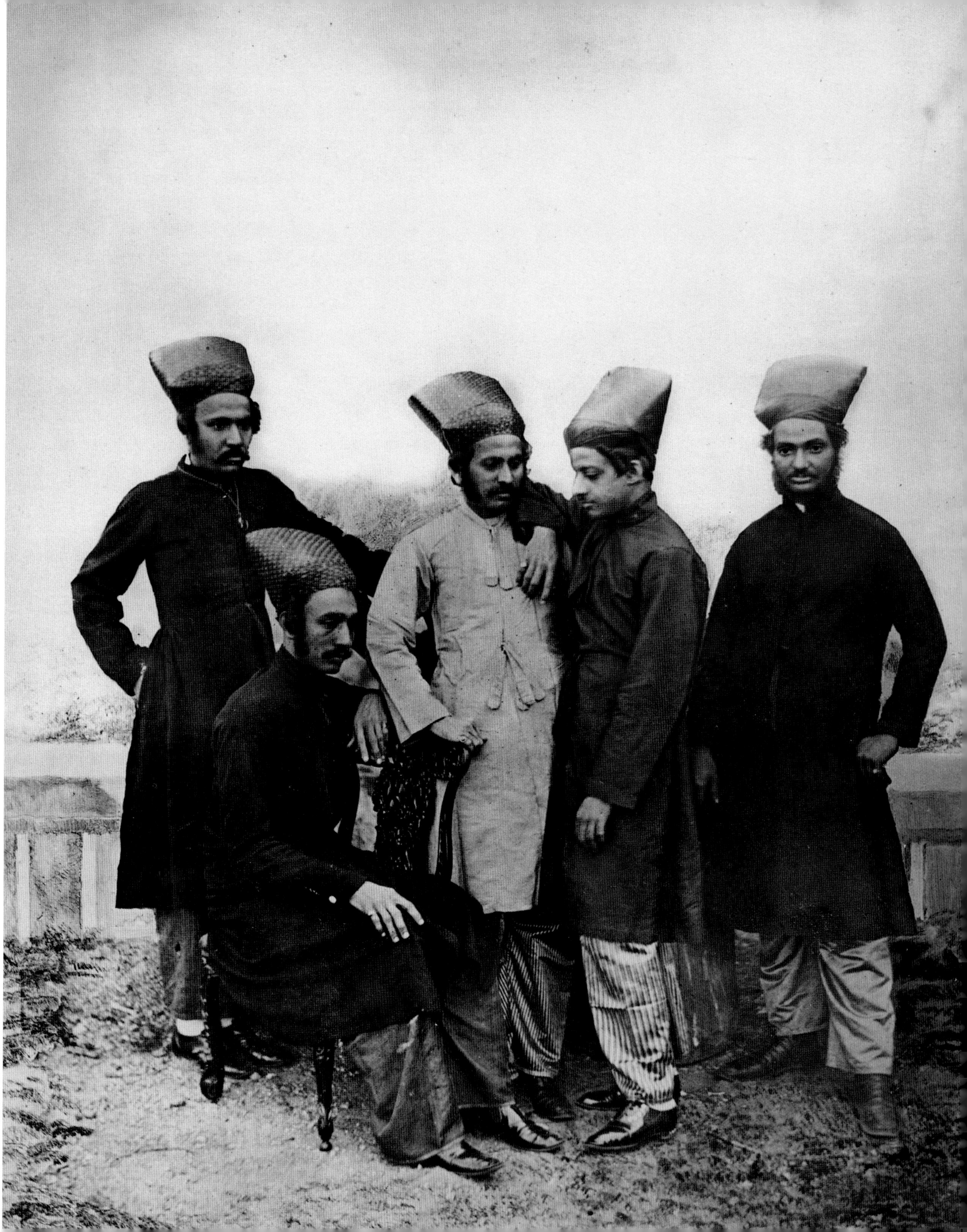

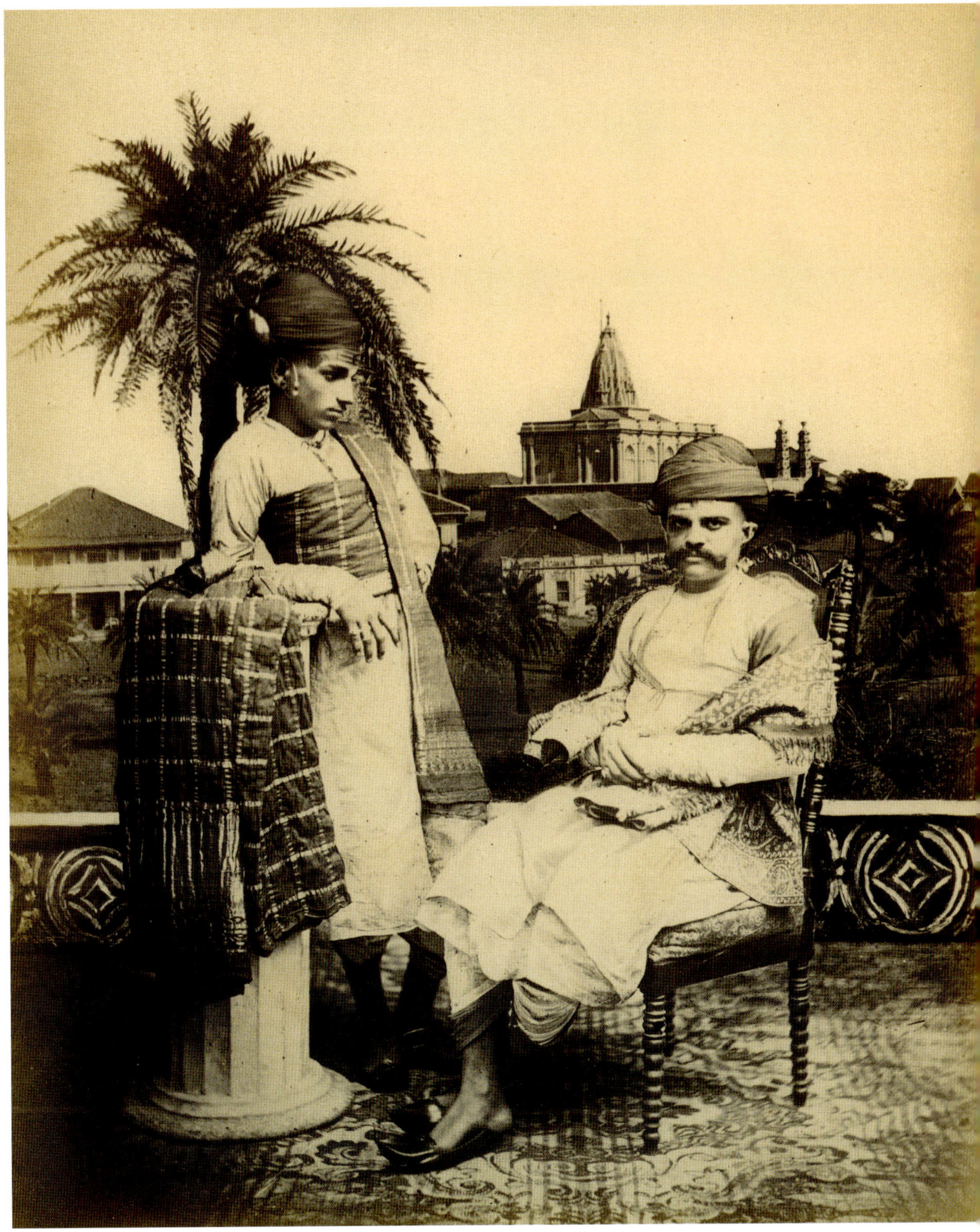

FACING PAGE

FIG. 20 | UNKNOWN PHOTOGRAPHER, POSSIBLY WILLIAM JOHNSON
*Parsis*
albumen silver print, 230 x 173 mm, c. 1863, from *The Oriental Races and Tribes, Residents and Visitors of Bombay* (Vol. I)
[ACP: D2005.67.0001 (87)]

FIG. 21 | UNKNOWN PHOTOGRAPHER, POSSIBLY WILLIAM JOHNSON
*Ghur Baree (House Holding) Gosaees*
albumen silver print, 230 x 177 mm, c. 1863, from *The Oriental Races and Tribes, Residents and Visitors of Bombay* (Vol. I)
[ACP: D2005.67.0001 (55)]

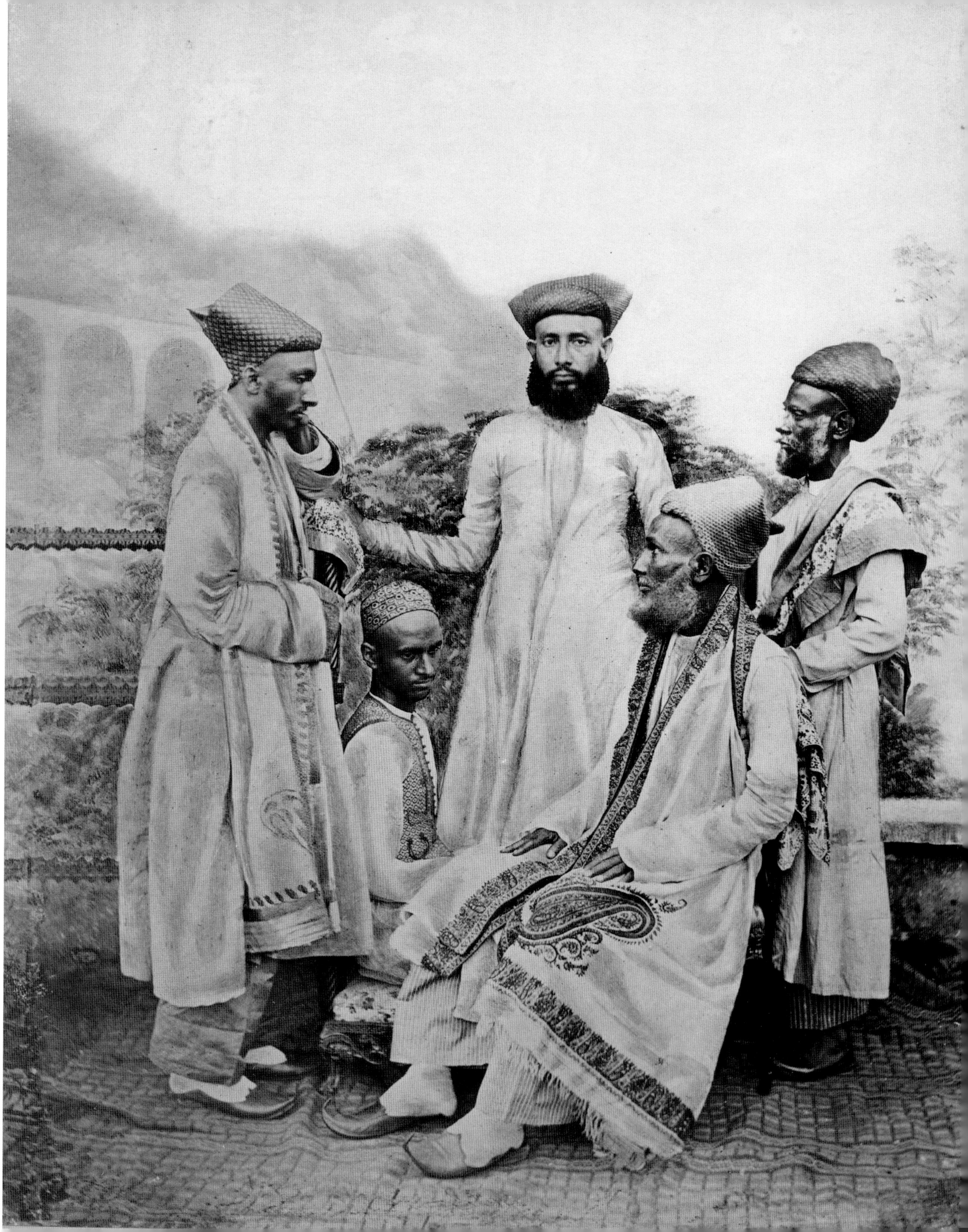

"The principal personage represented in our photograph is Fattih Singh Bhonsle, the brother of the Raja of Akalkot, a large jagirdar under the late Satara State. He is a young man of considerable activity, and was encouraged to stay in Bombay during the stirring time of the Great Mutiny…"[14]

In addition, the two individuals standing next to him are mentioned as his "Maratha attendants".[15] This peculiar engagement with the personal biography of ethnographic examples disturbs the universal objectivity of an ostensibly scientific project, infusing it with a dose of intrigue and even humour.

Further, while the theatrically absorbed gazes in *Parsis* (Fig. 20) may reflect a European tradition of artistic influence drawn from the lineage of history painting, the direct manner in which the gaze of the sitter meets the beholder in *Ghur Baree Gosaees* (Fig. 21), shows a contrary performative aesthetic, which only the novel space of the photographic studio could enable, making possibile the affirmation of identity by an emerging urban clientele.

Alongside display of the supposed racial, social and occupational signification, Johnson's albums actively emphasized manners of clothing and costumes as they might appear through cultural and/or religious affiliations. So, in contrast to later depictions of Muslim communities, and bearing in mind their widespread persecution following the Uprising of 1857,[16] the apparent focus of attention in *Mohammedans of Konkan* (Fig. 22) is on their beautifully flowing robes than anything else. Even *Roman Catholic Women of Salsette* (Fig. 23) gains appreciation for the costumes that the women adorn. The soft-toned backdrop in both examples brings attention back to the sitters and their attire rather than create a homology between the two, as is the case in Figure 17 and/or Figure 18.

## Conclusion

The work of Narayan Daji and William Johnson produced in Bombay during the 1860s is an immensely rich archive to excavate early precedents of photographic practice in the country, particularly in the field of ethnography and early anthropological photography. The quality of Daji's work and that of Johnson's composite prints, together with the ability to frame subjects in ways that overlapped visual as well as intellectual frames of reference, were remarkable for their time. Negotiated at the dawn of photography's increasing circulation in a burgeoning public sphere, their works were characterized by a playful, even intriguing liberty that have allowed the images to be read in different, even contrary ways. They went beyond the confines of what came to be associated with ethnographic photography. The works of later practitioners in the field became far more standardized as reflected in the production of the *People of India* series (1868–1875) which had a strictly museological emphasis along with remarks on civility and

FIG. 22 | UNKNOWN PHOTOGRAPHER, POSSIBLY WILLIAM JOHNSON
***Muhammadans of the Konkan***
albumen silver print, 229 x 177 mm, c. 1866, from *The Oriental Races and Tribes, Residents and Visitors of Bombay* (Vol. II)
[ACP: D2005.67.0001 (77)]

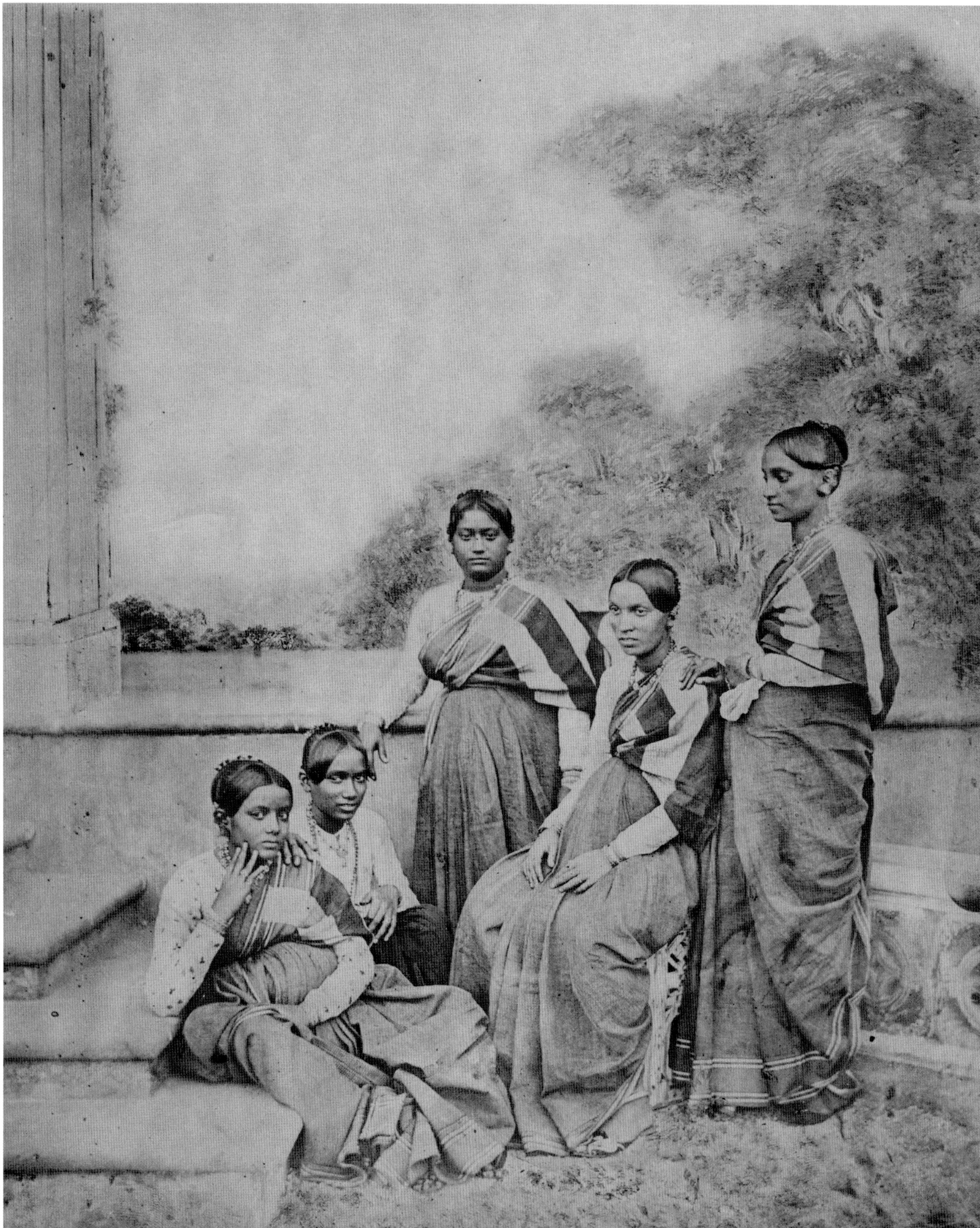

political loyalty to the British rule, on the heels of the Uprising of 1857. Along with further developments in the field of anthropology and the increasing emphasis on practices such as anthropometry, photography became even more restricted in the service of anthropologists. In comparison, the works of Daji and Johnson constituted much more than the precedents of ethnographic photography alone, drawing on a wider canvas of graphic arts and visual culture for a project ostensibly dedicated to scientific study and scholarship.

The photographs showcased as part of this exhibition offer a rare glimpse of the early precedents of a practice that aimed to capture the intangibility of identity through the lens of a positivist technology, albeit one that attempted this engagement in an open ended manner. Furthermore, they reflect the mode in which such images entered into a dialogue with other images, travelled and fed other narratives. The later existence of this genre and the conventions it anticipated would be propelled in a number of different trajectories—elucidated by Mitchell in the introductory quote to this essay—as the novelty of the technology diminished, to favour the preferences of anthropology as a disciplinary practice on the one hand, the market for the circulation of popular/sacred imagery on the other and the trends of studio photography celebrated by the urban elite at large.

NOTES

1 W.J.T. Mitchell, *What Do Pictures Want: The Lives and Loves of Images* (Chicago: The University of Chicago Press, 2005), 154.
2 A.K. Priyolkar, *Doctor Bhau Daji: Vyakti, Kal v Kartutwa—The man, his age and his work*, 1971
3 *ibid.*, frontispiece.
4 Notes compiled by John Falconer.
5 J. Falconer, *A Shifting Focus: Photography in India—1850–1900* (London: The British Library, 1995), 16.
6 *ibid.*
7 See C. Pinney, *Photos of the Gods The Printed Image and Political Struggle in India* (London: Reaktion Books, 2004).
8 K. Jain, "New Visual Technologies in the Bazaar: Reterritorialisation of the Sacred in Popular Print Culture", in *Sarai Reader 2003: Shaping Technologies*: 57.
9 Notes compiled by John Falconer.
10 William Johnson ed., *The Oriental Races and Tribes, Residents and Visitors of Bombay* Vol. 1 (London: W.J. Johnson, 1863), 9.
11 J. Falconer, *India: Pioneering Photographers 1850–1900* (London:The British Library and The Howard and Jane Ricketts Collection, 2001), 22.
12 Cf. N. Goodman, *Ways of Worldmaking* (Indianapolis: Hackett Publishing Co., 1978).
13 "General Remarks", *The Oriental Races and Tribes Residents and Visitors of Bombay* Vol. 1, ed. William Johnson (London: W.J. Johnson, 1863), 11–13.
14 See *The Oriental Races and Tribes, Residents and Visitors of Bombay* Vol. 1, ed. William Johnson, (London: W.J. Johnson, 1863), 37. See also C. Pinney, *Camera Indica: The Social Life of Indian Photographs* (London:Reaktion Books, 1997), 42–44, for another reference to personal biographies in the same album.
15 *ibid.*
16 Cf. *People of India*, a series of photographic albums produced between 1868–1875, which affirmed or questioned the political loyalty and/or civility of communities alongside photographs depicting members of the stated community.

FIG. 23 | UNKNOWN PHOTOGRAPHER, POSSIBLY WILLIAM JOHNSON
*Roman Catholic Women of Salsette*
albumen silver print, 228 x 177 mm, c. 1866, from *The Oriental Races and Tribes, Residents and Visitors of Bombay* (Vol. II) [ACP: D2005.67.0001 (95)]

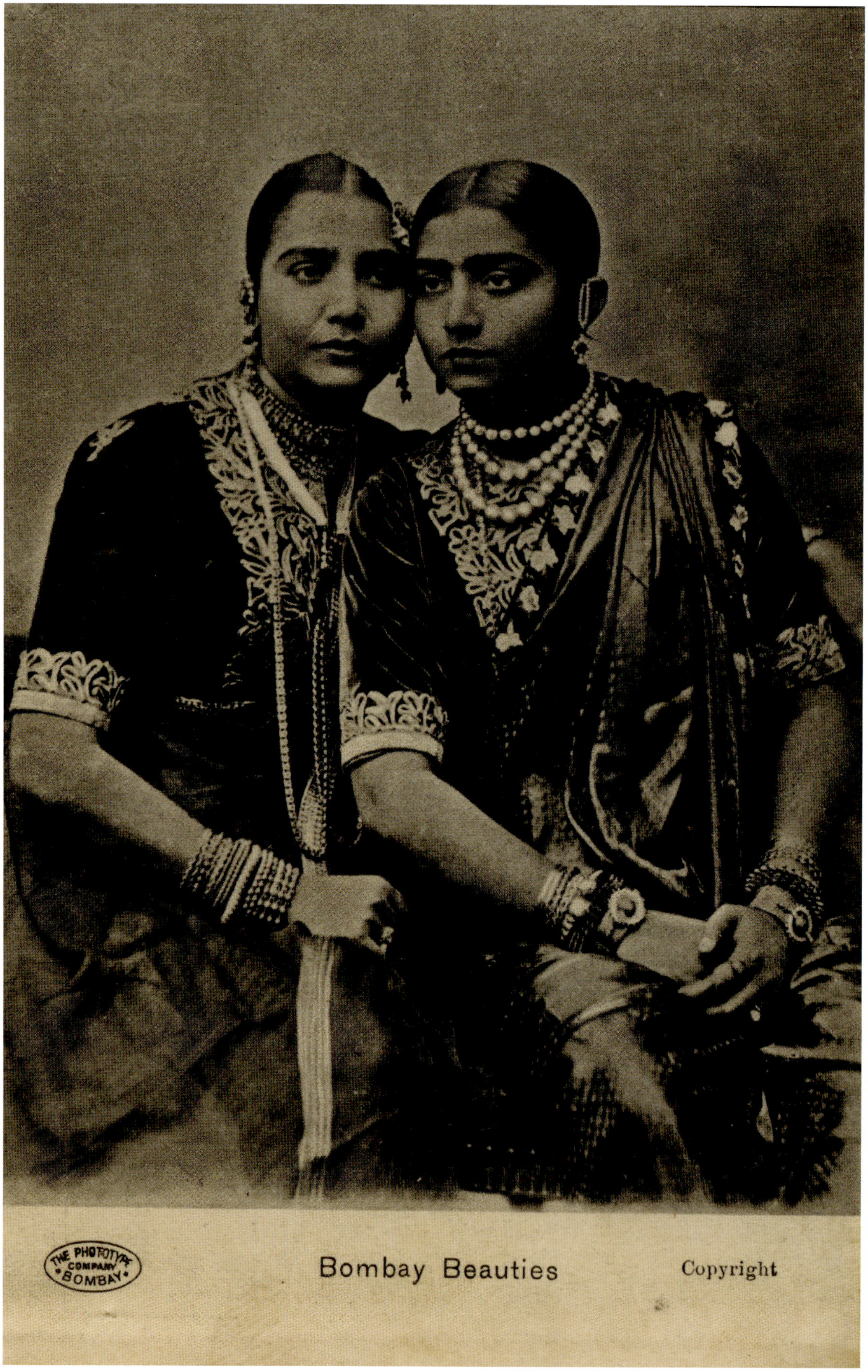

THE PHOTOTYPE COMPANY BOMBAY

Bombay Beauties

# Facing the Lens
## Women in Bombay's Photographic Studios

Suryanandini Sinha

Gendered identities in photographic studios capture the essence of this exhibition, by drawing attention to the intricacies of portraiture in India. Women as particular subjects in studios throughout the subcontinent and even in Bombay [now Mumbai] have had a perceptible relationship with the photographic visual; the processes and internal dynamics of image taking are specific to their social and sexual identities. While each photographic studio may have its own history of technology, aesthetics, expertise and clientele, a large sample of images such as these merits a thematic examination of the conventional tropes used to position women as subjects of the lens and incarnations of larger sociological concerns.

Women have been the subjects of studio photography ever since the medium's inception, embodying many complexities of representation through a century-and-half of photographic history in India. Questions and revelations abound in these images, and hence I seek to analyze some of the first samples of studio photos that foreground women, in order to diagnose how gender also conditions the dynamics of visuality. While studio photography, since the early-twentieth century, has undergone much technological change, it traces its roots to the initial aesthetics that emerged at the inception of the medium, while it was still used outside the precincts and purposes of the studio. I seek to elaborate here, some part of the wider history pertinent to studio photography in India, together with significant theoretical possibilities presented by the portrait photos of women.

The year 1840 saw India's first camera in the city of Calcutta [now Kolkata]. With the headquarters of the English East India Company located here, the city became the site from where the British commissioned professionals to take daguerreotype images surveying the Indian landscape and architecture. This was followed by country-wide anthropometric portraits of the various Indian native "types" that featured in projects such as the eight-volume the *People of India* series (1868–1875) containing more than 400 mounted prints. The camera was hence used to document different castes and tribes of the Indian populace, either for fear of their extinction or rebellion against the Empire. Photography thus developed a vocabulary that aided the discipline in both academic and, more strongly, political ways to seek order and gain control in an unfamiliar cultural and social fabric. Ethnographic photography emerged as the precedent to studio-based photography, and carried over some of its technical and aesthetic vocabulary as well.

FIG. 24 | BOMBAY PHOTOTYPE CO.
*Bombay Beauties*
postcard, 139 x 87mm, c. 1910,
printed in Luxemburg [ACP: 2001.15.1197]

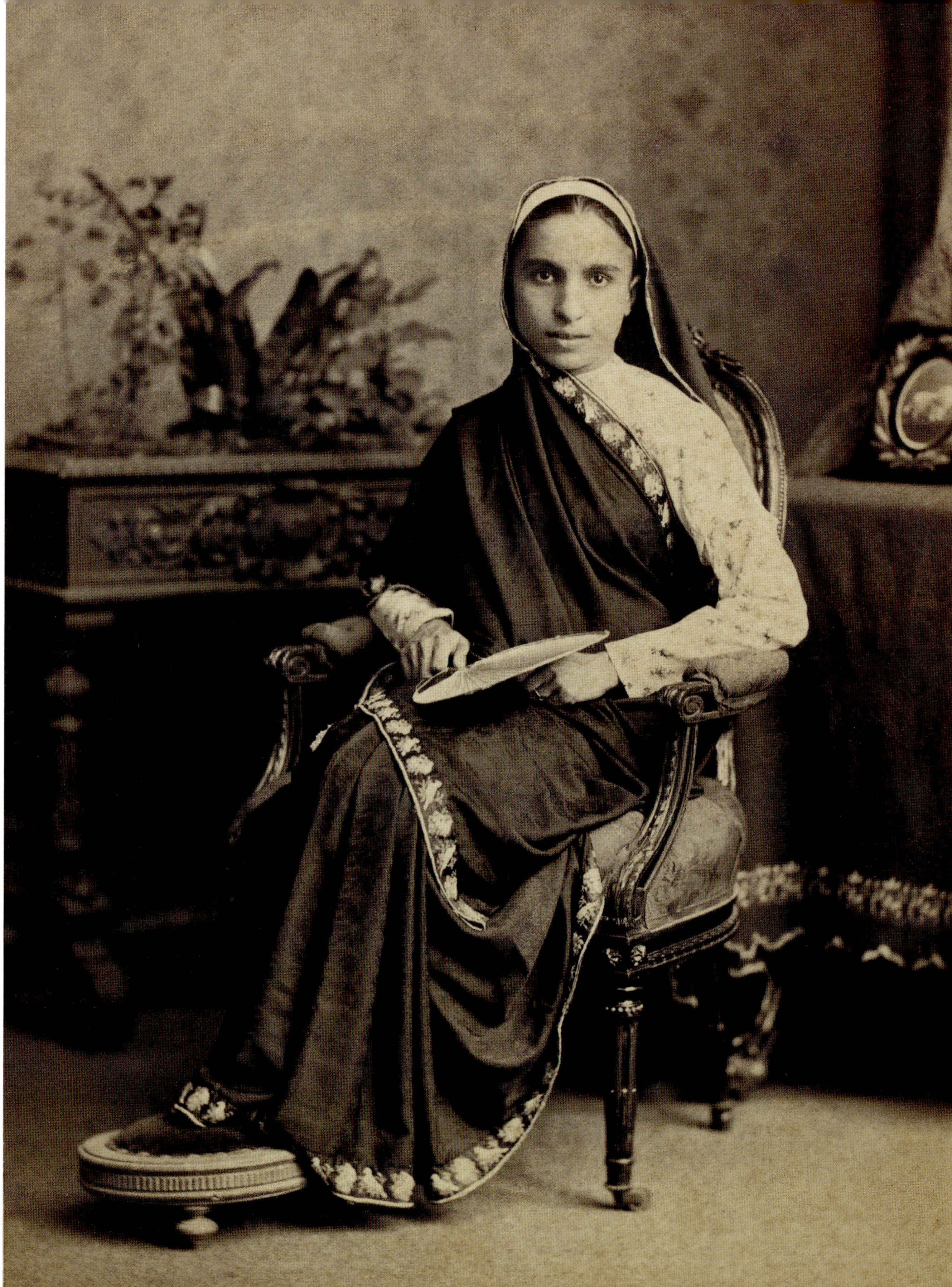

Bourne & Shepherd SIMLA, CALCUTTA & BOMBAY.

Photos of Indians were hence taken through both organised and amateur initiatives, contributing to what the visual anthropologist Christopher Pinney has called a "living museum of mankind", enshrining persons in visual frames that permanently located them in terms of their religious, regional and caste attributes. He says, with reference to the women in the *People of India* series, "... this quest for difference tended to make the women of a group more interesting, since their costume and material culture were identified as being more resistant to change."[1] Indian women in conjunction with their caste affiliation were thus perceived as the anchors of cultural groups, most immutable in the hierarchy of "natives"—and fixed as such in the photographic survey of the country.

In ethnographic portraits, women occupied a space of scrutiny and classification, but beyond the documentary function, they also came to be photographed for voyeuristic interests, and they were made to model as entertainers or nautch girls for postcards. These would circulate as souvenirs among male audiences of Indian and foreign origin (Fig. 24). They would typically be figured in a dance pose such as this, self consciously flaunting their costume and jewellery and circulated on the surfaces of cards with nomenclatures alluding to their profession.

### Home-grown Studios

The significant point of departure for studios was their role in the creation of imagery for the sitters themselves i.e. in locally owned and operated studios that harboured aesthetics borrowed from portrait painting. Samuel Bourne (1834–1912), a visiting British photographer, was one of the first to take individual initiative with regard to the new visual medium, and he set up a photo studio in 1864 in Calcutta that was a forerunner in its trade, followed by the one in Bombay in 1870 (Fig. 25). While he was instrumental in establishing prototypes of postures, props and mannerisms in portraits such as these, which were heavily replicated by other studios, he wrote that he was not alone, and that Indian photographers led by Lala Deen Dayal also took to studio photography by the 1870s[2] presenting both similar and unique aesthetics. Sophie Gordon has written with regard to the late-nineteenth century scenario, "... small studios catering to a middle-class clientele were able to flourish in towns across the country, catering to a largely Indian market, resulting often in a visual language that saw painted backdrops and European props such as a chair and table with a vase of flowers or perhaps a pile of books, combined with techniques such as collage and the hand painting of portraits ... the act of having a portrait taken, as well as the studio setting, was a way of demonstrating status and creating an identity".[3]

Bombay was a forerunner in catering to photographic needs of its public, and studios were clustered in several parts of the city as organized ventures, to compose portraits of individuals and groups. The studio became more than a site for image production in the days of the Raj. It was a temporary space of occupation that enclosed potential for the transformation of the mundane into

FIG. 25 | BOURNE & SHEPHERD
*Portrait of a Seated Parsi Lady*
albumen print, 165 x 107 mm, c. 1880–1890
[ACP: 95.0037 (25)]

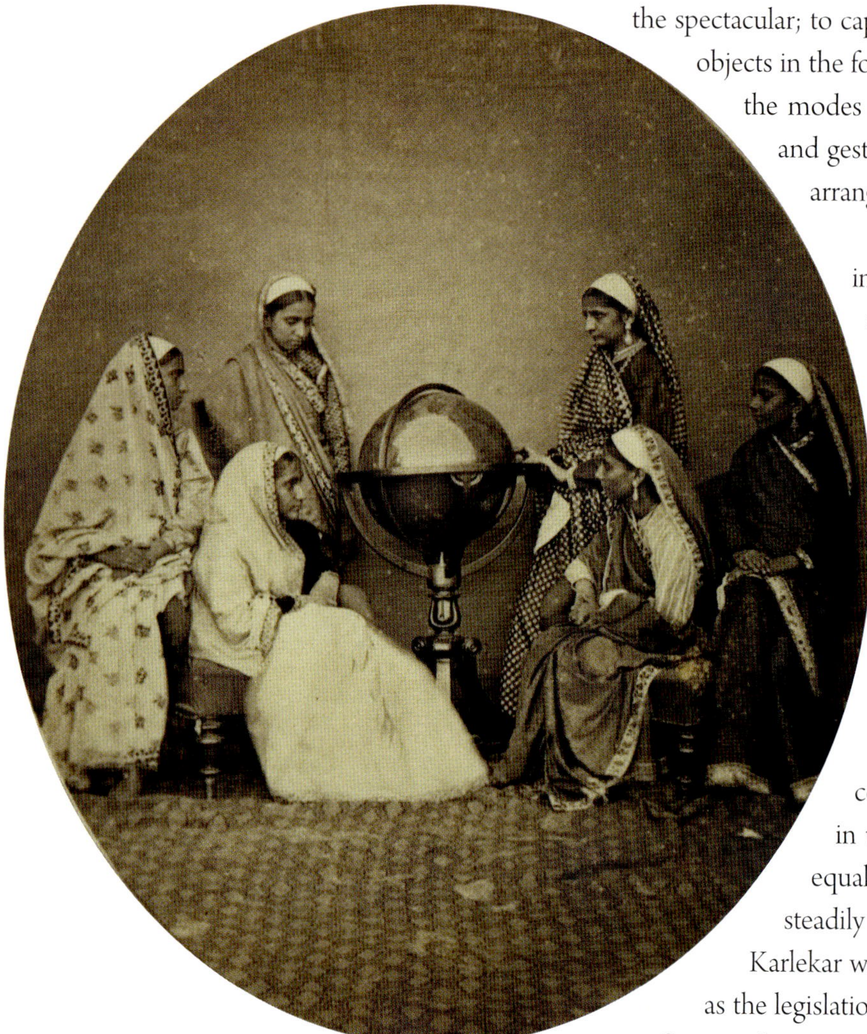

the spectacular; to capture the latter on lens and then release the frozen moments as tangible objects in the form of photos back into the hubbub of everyday living. It came to house the modes of such transformation in the physical form of imaginative sets, props and gestures and the aesthetics of self devised or borrowed, sociologically laden arrangements of subjects.

Over the years, even as access to the camera became democratized in India, with handheld cameras profusely available in the market, the status of the photo studio remained unquestioned for the most important images. These pertained to ceremonial or ritual occasions and images of identification. The multitude of photographic studios over rural and urban India today, reflect the widespread desire for the Indian public to confirm the supremacy of the professional photographer. This is also reflected in Pierre Bourdieu's study of middle class peasantry in France, where he says, "the photographer is considered to know his job and no-one else has any point of comparison ... no one (in a family photograph) would think of disobeying the photographer's instructions, of talking to neighbours, or looking in the other direction ..."[4]

Historically, while the late-nineteenth and early-twentieth centuries had seen women perform the important role of photographers in the *zenana* studios, this was a trend that declined with growing sexual equality and social freedoms of women. Visibility of women without *purdah* steadily declined to be socially prohibited. Gender studies theorist Malavika Karlekar writes of the rise of education and social reforms favouring women, such as the legislations banning sati, child marriage and infanticide during the early decades of twentieth century, which encouraged their freedom in the visual domain as well[5] (Fig. 26). In this image, a group of Parsi girls sit in a highly directed group, stiff and still, yet looking at the promise radiating from large central globe, suggestive of the liberation and hope that education offered them.

FIG. 26 | UNKNOWN PHOTOGRAPHER
*Pupils and staff of the Alexandra Native Girls Institution*
albumen silver print, 126 x 98 mm, 1874, from *Alexandra English Institution 1867* album
[ACP: 95.0036 (02)]

Karlekar also elucidates the case of the ordinary woman in pre-Independent India as having been relatively less individualized in portrait photographs. Their portraits hence appeared embedded in family albums, and most often they were photographed with their husbands or children, rather than appearing alone (Figs 27 and 28). Here, the women from a Parsi family are arranged around the central matriarchal figure, with two girls in stylized postures at her feet granting symmetry and stability to the group form. In contrast, the Borah family has a small bejewelled girl child at its centre, as she is still exempt from the conventions of the veil that other women in the family may usually follow, with exception granted for the photographic moment.

FACING PAGE
FIG. 27 | LALA DEEN DAYAL (*attribution*)
*Parsee Women: Bombay*
albumen silver print, 254 x 201 mm, c. 1900
[ACP: 94.08.0060]

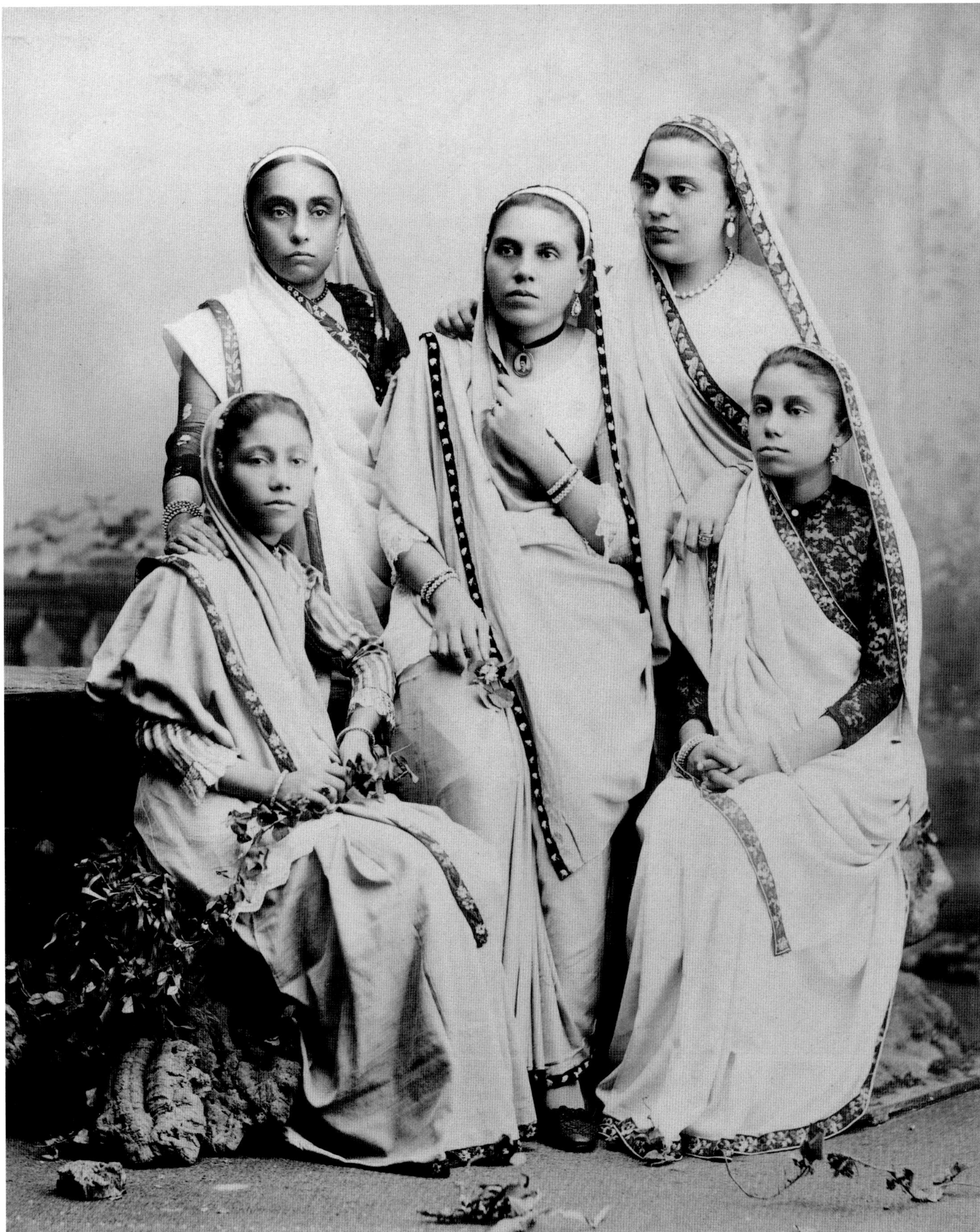

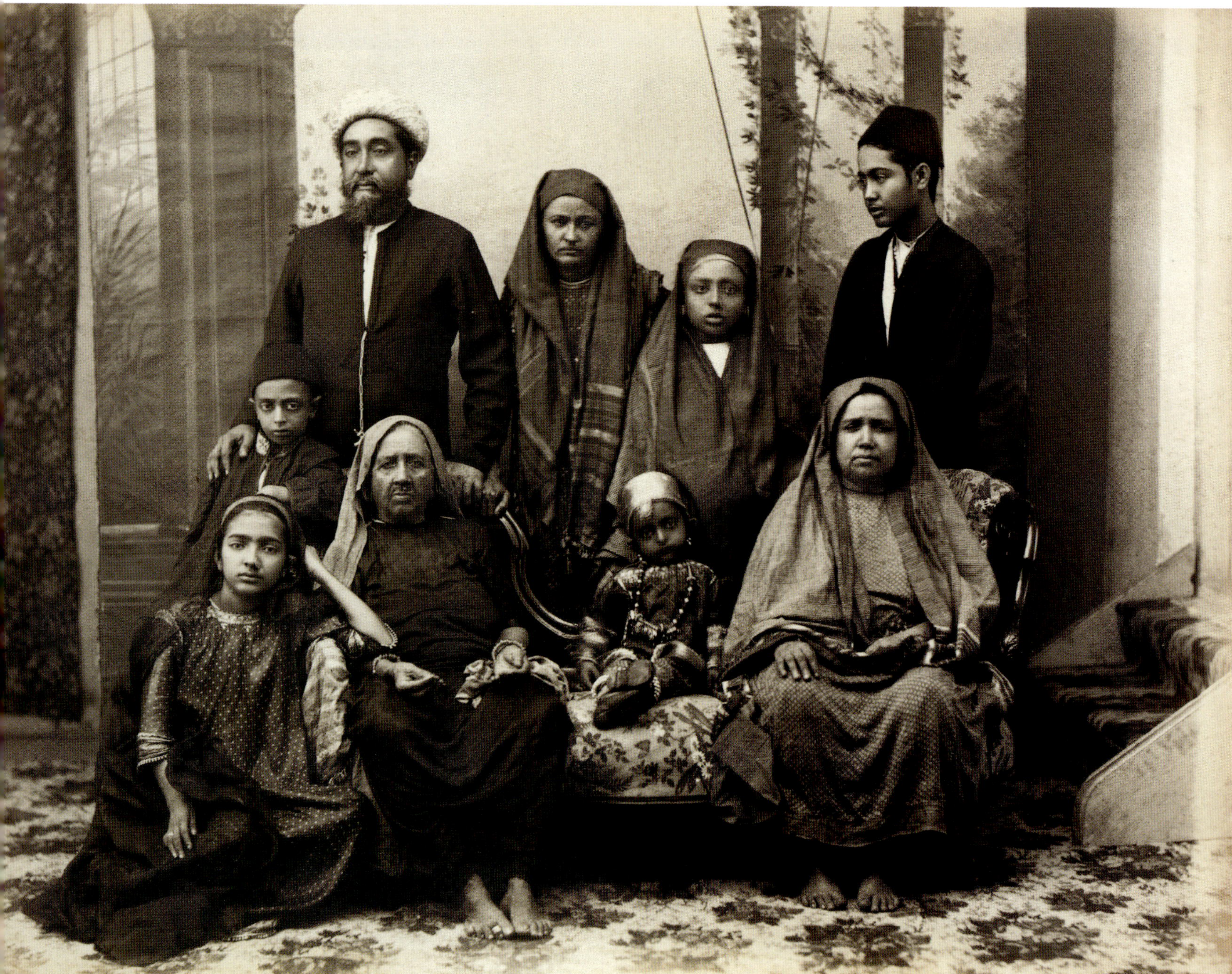

FIG. 28 | UNKNOWN PHOTOGRAPHER
*A Borah Family*
albumen silver print, 182 x 233 mm, c. 1880–1890
[ACP: 94.66.0023]

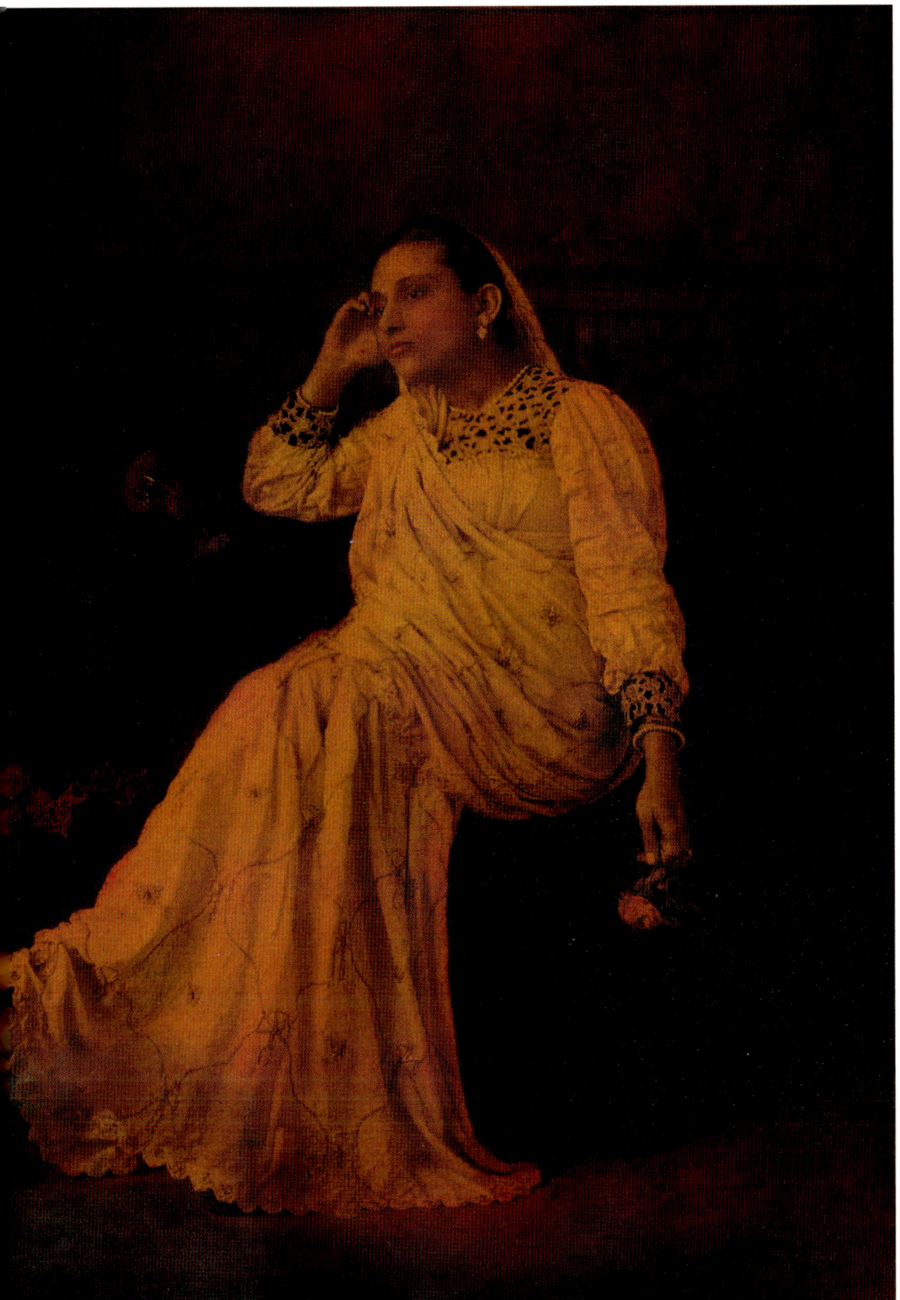

FIG. 29 | UNKNOWN PHOTOGRAPHER;
UNKNOWN ARTIST
*Parsi Lady*
gelatin silver print and watercolour,
285 x 205 mm, c. 1920 [ACP: D2003.32.0020]

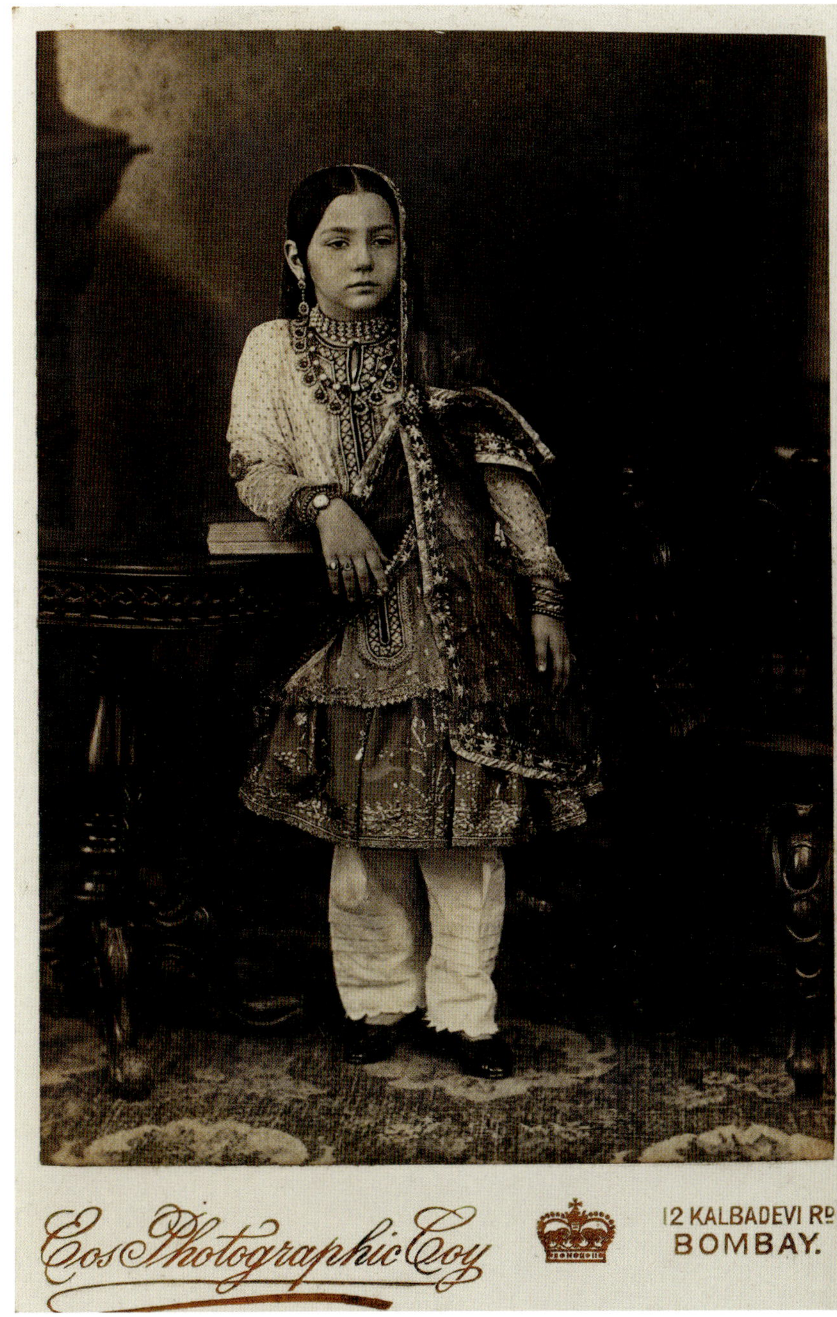


FIG. 30 | EOS PHOTOGRAPHIC COMPANY
*Portrait of a Young Girl*
albumen cabinet card, 139 x 98 mm,
c. 1880–1890s [ACP: 95.0037 (02)]

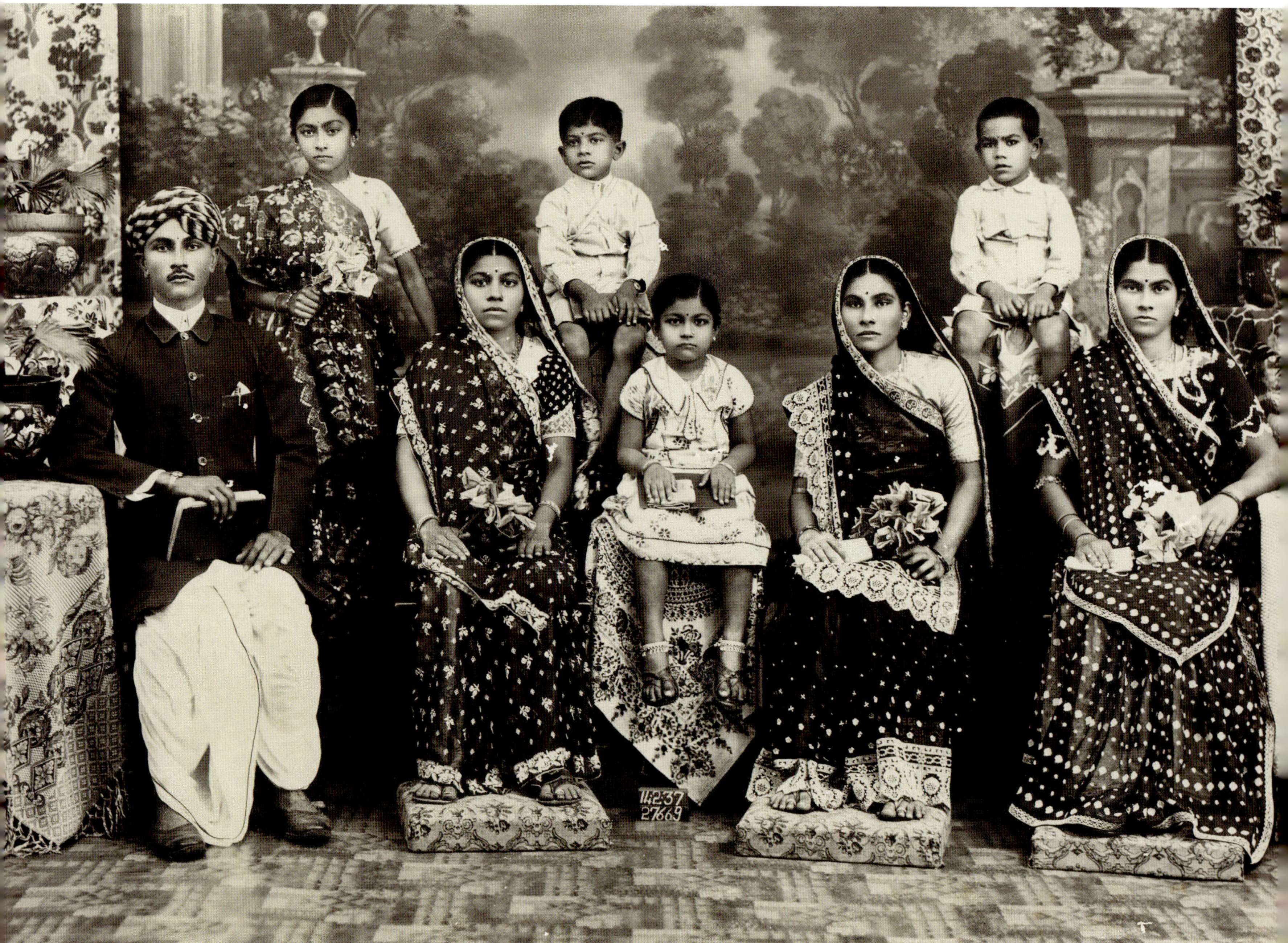
14.2.37
27669

For a long time, individual photographs of women pertained mostly to royalty and nobility, which were sophisticated portraits for posterity, coexisting with or even replacing portrait painting. Gradually, photography became the ordinary man's portrait as it became relatively more affordable, and even resembled portrait painting in multiple ways, for instance when portrait photos were conjoined seamlessly with traditional miniature painting. Christopher Pinney, Judith Mara Gutman and Samuel Bourne in their writings note how hand tinting had been used to embellish the early portraits, highlighting jewellery and clothing with resplendent paint (Fig. 29). Photography also catered to a more personal and plebian variety of individual portraiture in the form of cabinet cards or cartes-de-visite (Fig. 30). Women were most often photographed waist upwards and images were pasted on card measuring 4.5 x 2.5 inches for cartes-de-visite or 6.25 x 4.25 inches for cabinet cards. These were personal mementos presented by both men and women, to their relatives and friends. Curiously, they never bore the name of the sitter printed on either the front or the back, but were always embossed with or had the name of the photo studio that took the portrait. Hence, visual identification and memory were considered to be adequate tools for remembrance, and textual reference for name or title was not considered necessary—a phenomenon that is reversed in contemporary times in the concept of visiting cards.

## Alternative Aesthetics

Photographs that were taken by the local population of and for themselves, were hence made with a different intent by colonial photographers, and accordingly varied in style and content. These portraits occupied the space between private and public visual domains, as a presentation of the self to a select or general public with inclusions and accretions from the material world that defined one's existence. Hence, elaborate studio backdrops and objects that accrued status to the subjects came to replace their tools that had alluded to caste. The photo studios became arenas of dreams and aspired wealth and beauty, obliterating occupational and economic particularities and downplaying "ethnicity" of subjects in the face of fantastic spectacles. From the end of the nineteenth century, painted backdrops ranging from scenic beauty to Indian monuments or palatial interiors came to be used profusely. Still prevalent in studios of small towns in India, these backdrops are significant for the sitters who would never themselves travel to the location on display (Fig. 31). Here there is the dreamy landscape in the background, ornate pillars and vases on the sides and noticeably, footstools for the bouquet-bearing ladies of the family.

There was, what Bourdieu describes as the concept of "social" roles within which women were photographed—such as wife, mother, sister, or daughter. The portraits of couples (Fig. 32) demonstrate a clear choreography with either the man or the woman seated on a chair, or both seated side-by-side with a definite use of backdrops depicting interior spaces. The architecture in the background usually drew from European buildings or theatrical sets, and the furniture used

FIG. 31 | POSSIBLY D. NUSERWANJI, BOMBAY
*Hindu Family Portrait*
gelatin silver print, 205 x 285 mm,
11 February 1937
Photographer's Reference: 27669
[ACP: D2003.11.0007]

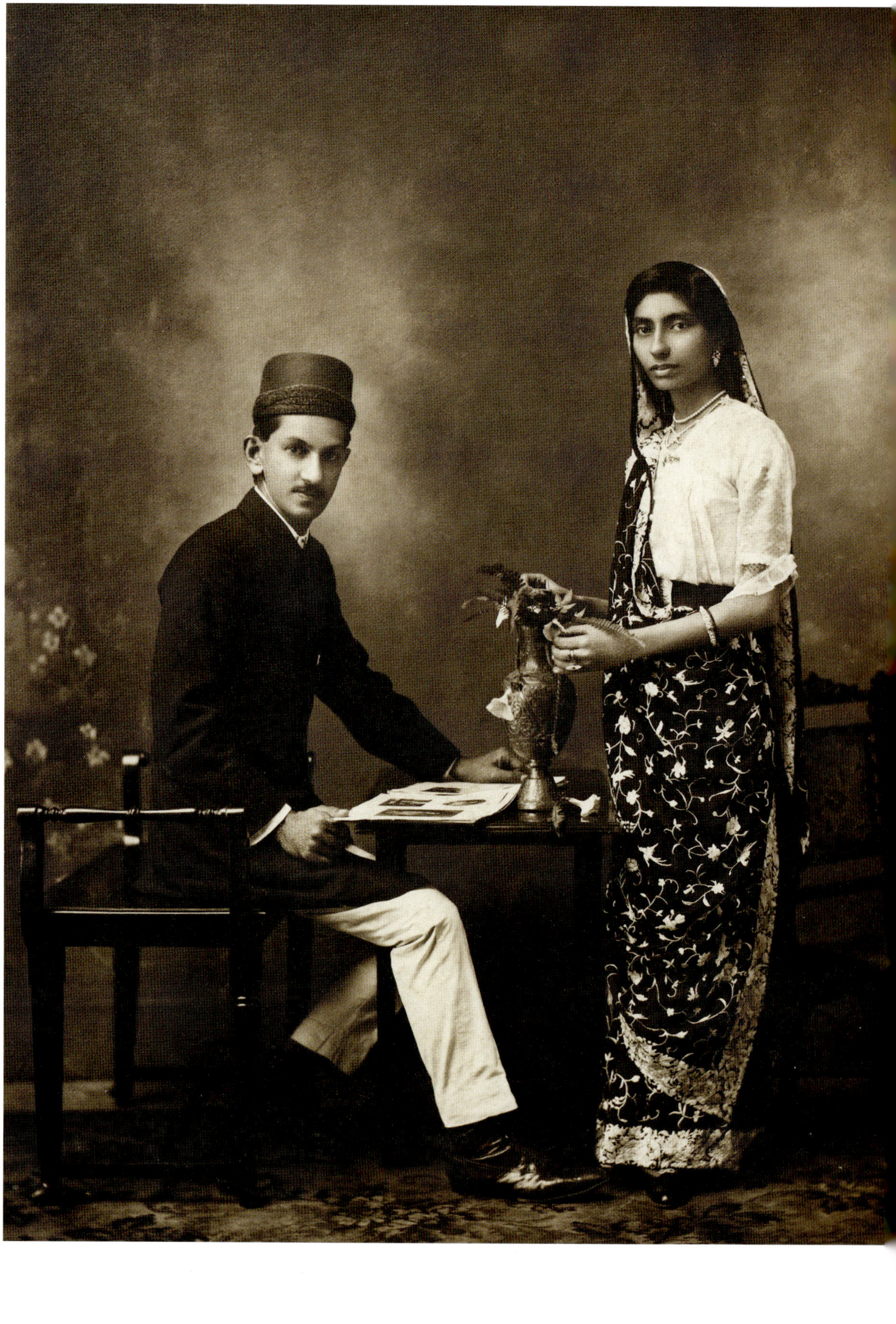

FIG. 32 | GOMES & LAWRIE
*Portrait of a Parsi Couple*
gelatin silver print, 203 x 150 mm, c. 1940s
[ACP: D2003.32.0026]

FACING PAGE
FIG. 33 | NATIONAL PHOTO STUDIO
*Portrait of Mother and Daughter*
gelatin silver print, 202 x 155 mm, c. 1940s
[ACP: D2003.23.0025]

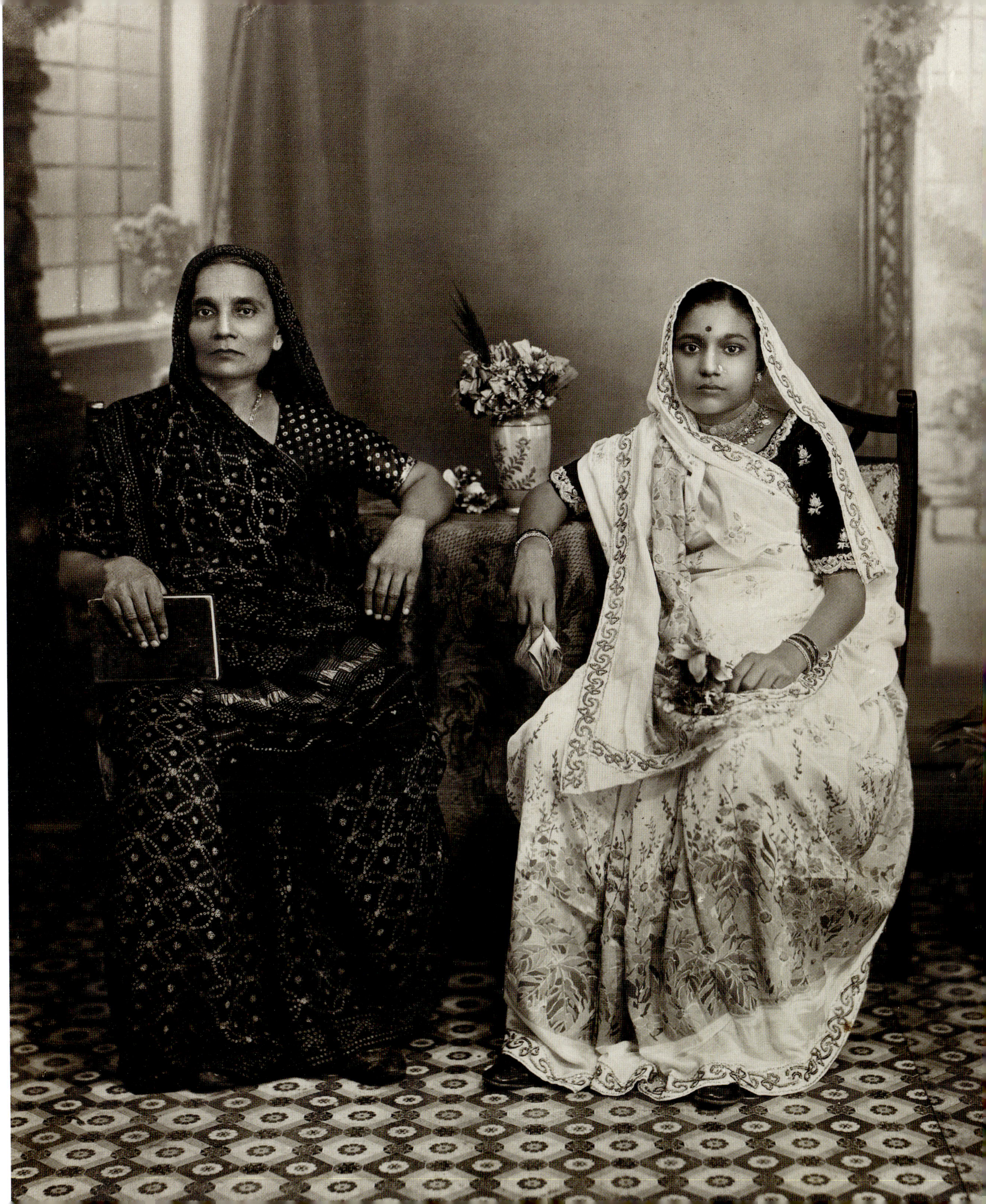

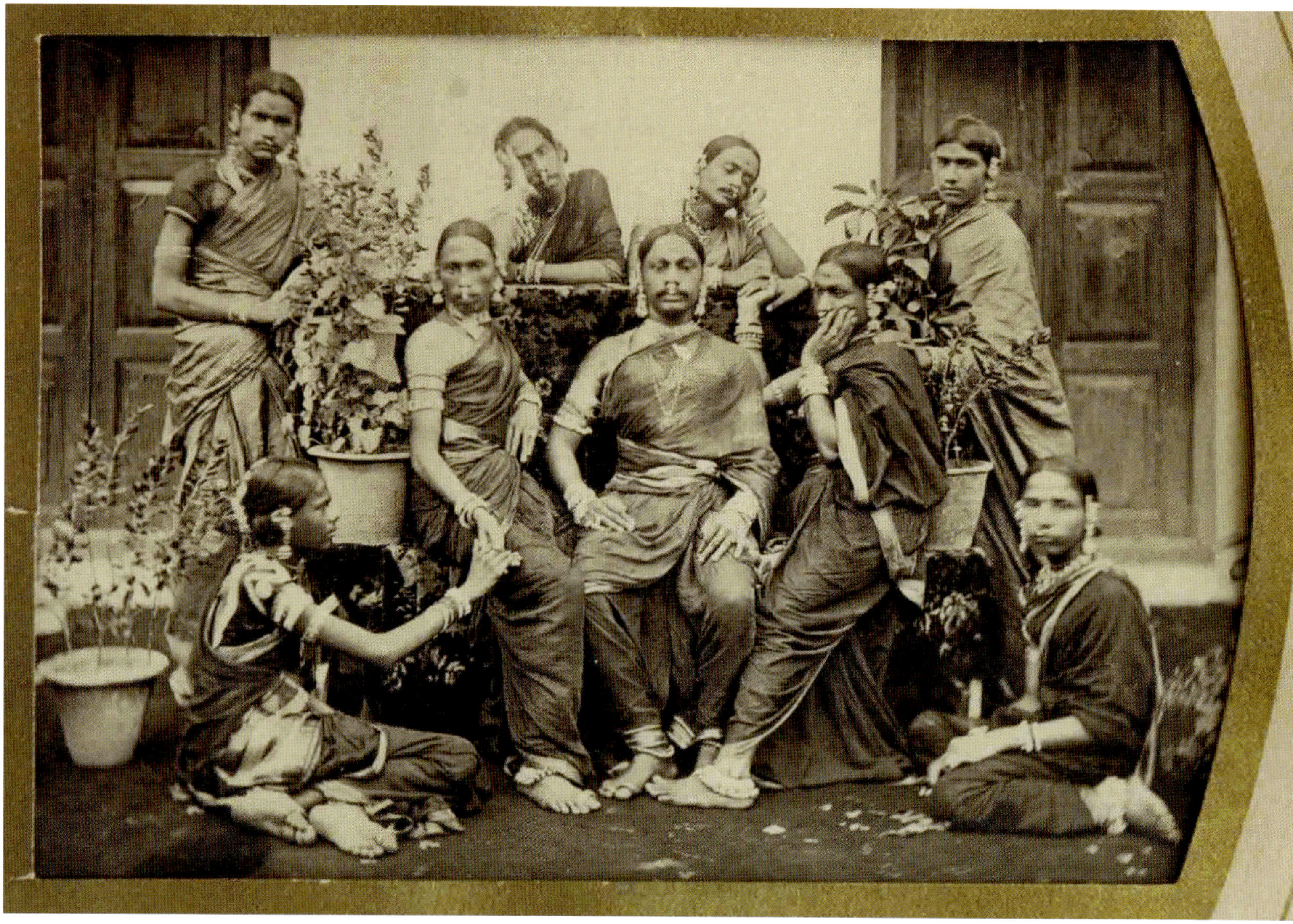

FIG. 34 | CHUNNI LAL BHAWANI RAM
*Hijras*
albumen print, 100 x 190 mm (approx), c. 1880s
[ACP: 2008.02.0004 (06)]

in the studio in the form of chairs, footstools and pillars were also of Western design. The hands of the figures would either be lying on their laps, clearly in the field of vision, or engaged in bearing objects suited to their status and sex—objects such as a book for the man and a flower vase for his wife. The effort for the studio and its photographer was thus to exceed the purpose of indexicality[6] that had previously imbued anthropometric portraits, and enter the realms of iconicity, making the sitter look "more" or "better" than she was (evoking the observations made by Pinney[7]).

The variety of portraits encapsulating two persons, other than the conjugal portraits, were those of women, usually sisters, or mother and daughter, with the younger woman standing while the elder one is seated on a chair. Both may be holding objects such as flowers or handkerchiefs, although the older woman would often be distinguished by a book or fan (Fig. 33).

In conclusion, one can dwell on the readings that photos from studios can present with reference to the public and private lives of sitters. Studios function as spaces for the portrayal of hierarchical relations within the family, locating women in positions of power or submission according to the delineations of social custom. On the one hand, family photographs, displayed in households and albums ossify the relations that are projected in the arrangement of figures, as standing or seated, front or back row, reaffirming, but also often introducing hierarchies. On the other hand, these same relations and positions activate the personae of women and locate their identities in a larger social realm. Pictured alone, women often refer to an absent presence, either by markers of dress or the objects they bear, situating them socially as married or unmarried, classifying them as ladies of an elite social segment or nautch girls for a male audience.

A unique function of the studio lies in its potential to touch the realm of imagination. Positioning women with books, musical instruments and fantastic backdrops, they exceed reality in representation. It is of interest to note, however, that in the studio, fantasy too is conventionalized. Props, backdrops and postures are repetitively used in the studio space to release only so many possible portraits to clients. Such is the fate also of the intriguing figures of eunuchs (*hijras*) in the Alkazi Collection, taken by Chunni Lal Bhawani Ram in the 1880s, who appear to have a mixed identity, as entertainers and objects of sexual interest (Fig. 34). Their figures are palpable with the desire of perhaps appearing overtly effeminate in their fluid postures and artfully arranged limbs. The directness of their gazes is countered by the ambiguity of their status, the studio being the stage that conceals equally as it reveals. The tension then is between the studio's role as possible liberator or controller, and whether the frame packs in a figure with centripetal force or whether it releases its contents with centrifugal energies. What women can embody is a certain flexibility of meaning, mobile in their positioning and their acquired significance in relation to the objects or people who surround them, while also allowing the beholder's vision with the freedom to imagine.

NOTES

1 Christopher Pinney, *Camera Indica* (London: Reaktion Books Ltd, 1997), 29.

2 Samuel Bourne, "Photography in the East," *British Journal of Photography* (July 1863).

3 "The Colonial Project and the Shifting Gaze," in *Indian Art and Visual Culture—1857–2000*, ed. Gayatri Sinha (Mumbai and New Delhi: Marg Publications with National Culture Fund and Bodhi Art, 2009).

4 Pierre Bourdieu, *Photography, a Middle Brow Art* (Stanford: Stanford University Press, 1996), 22.

5 Malavika Karlekar ed., *Visualizing Indian Women—1875–1947* (New Delhi: Oxford University Press, 2005).

6 C. S. Pierce identified indexes to be one of the three types of "signs", which could alternatively be symbols and icons. Indexical signs are those which have some natural relationship of contiguity with their referent. The indexicality of a photograph is confirmed by the physical act of light bouncing off an object through the lens of a camera and onto the filmic emulsion which leaves the trace that becomes the image (Pinney 1997, 20).

7 Christopher Pinney, *Camera Indica* (London: Reaktion Books Ltd, 1997), 178.

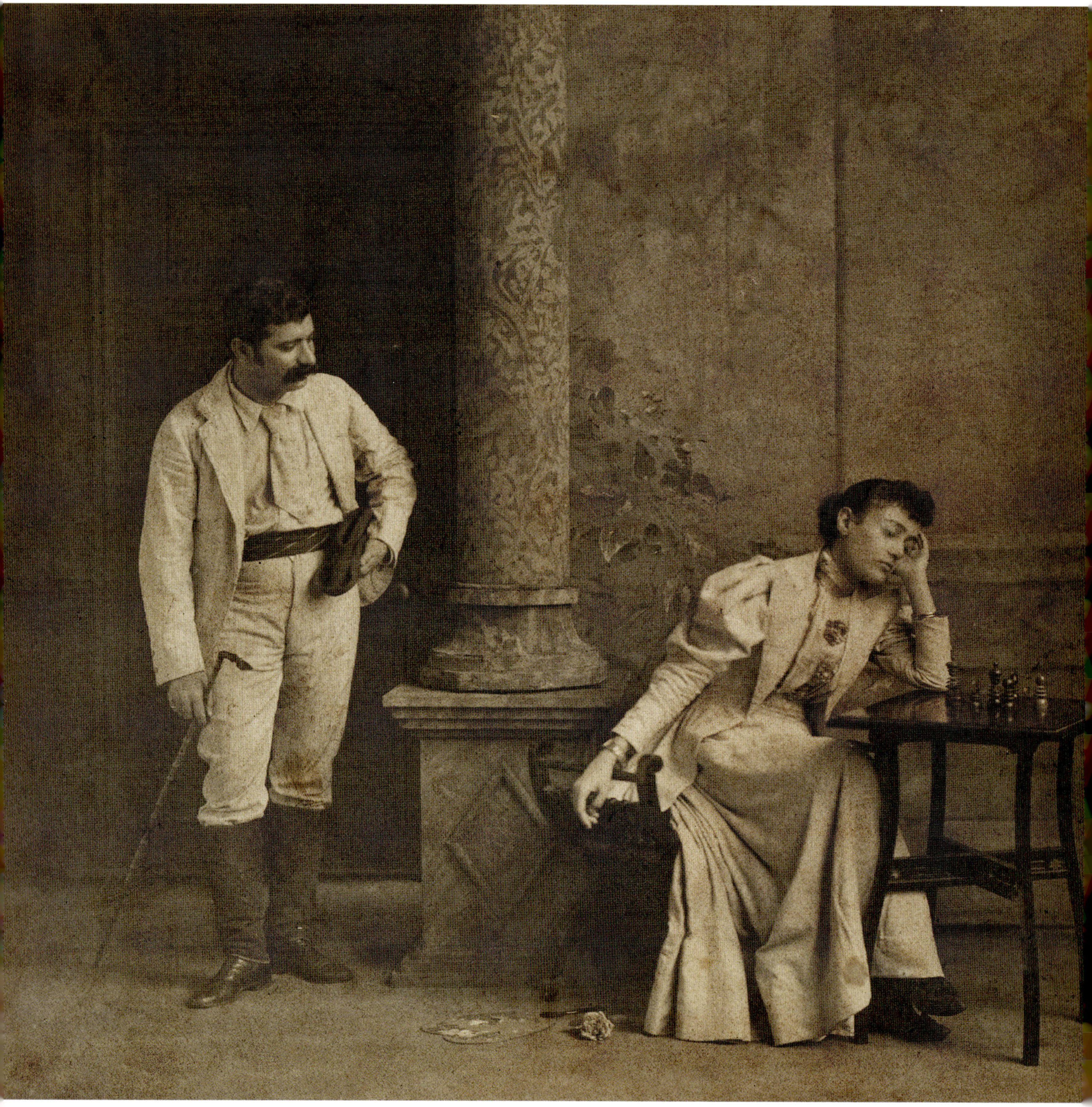

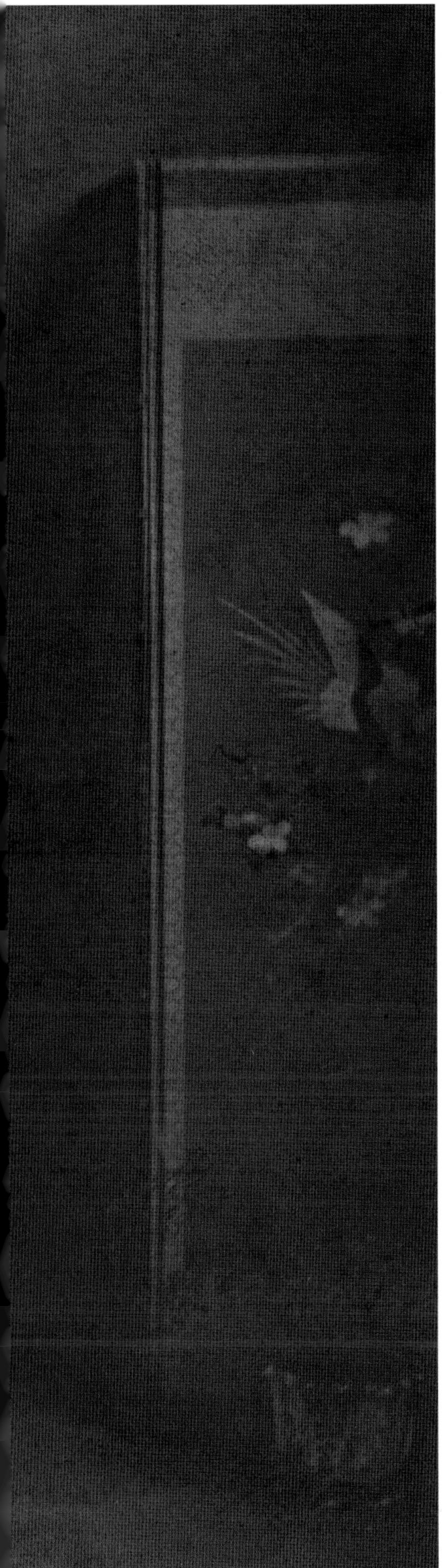

# Performance for Camera
## Shapoor N. Bhedwar and the Dimensions of Studio Photography in Bombay

Rahaab Allana

Light and expression are perhaps the two principal elements infused in the creation of a strong portrait. To aesthetically manage the luminosity upon the sitter, and thereby accentuate his/her character, were central components for the production of sepia-toned depictions in the nineteenth century. Though, just as these artistic means were essential requisites for proclaiming a handsome likeness, so too was the space in which the cameraman endeavoured to coax his clientele to their fullest, photogenic potential. Interestingly, in the mid-nineteenth century, photographic studios appeared as portable galleries and improvised quarters, ranging from pushcarts, horse-drawn vans to flatboats and railroad cars. They contained a minimal area to pose the sitter, a camera, which in late-nineteenth century would have been the revolutionary Eastman Kodak No.1, a darkroom to sensitize the plates and another adjoining space to prepare and mount finished prints.[1] One of the most important elements here was the need for natural illumination, which was more often provided by a skylight. Studios located in buildings, therefore, had to be placed on the top floor. In order to minimise the effect of the intensity and quality of changing light from morning to noon and then dusk, mirrors and reflectors were used to focus the glow upon the subject (Fig. 35).

The expansion of such studios in India began with the arrival of equipment to the ports, the most active of which were the cities of Bombay and Calcutta [now Mumbai and Kolkata respectively]. As is the case today, Bombay was a commercially driven metropolis, and photography became a means of bridging the linked fields of patronage and industry, displaying a vast cultural tapestry of its people. With rising commerce and trade, the need for sophisticated studios steadily increased in order to pander to the shifting tastes of those who wished to be celebrated by the lens. A vast canvas of society from all walks saw themselves magically imprinted on paper, and with time, photography was no longer treated as an isolated form of documentation or surveillance, but rather a means for articulating a palpable correlation between the arts. The following essay is therefore an attempt to value the studio as a liberating and convivial space, wherein the union of conjecture and culture allowed for an evolving visual vocabulary at the turn of the nineteenth century.

In this context, the exhibition presents the work of a provocative wielder of the medium, Shapoor N. (Nusserwanji?) Bhedwar, through his unique album now in the Alkazi Collection

PAGES 56–57
FIG. 35 | SHAPOOR N. BHEDWAR
*Mate in Three Moves*
carbon print, 263 x 342 mm, c. 1890s, from *Art Studies* album
[ACP: 97.47.0001 (05)]

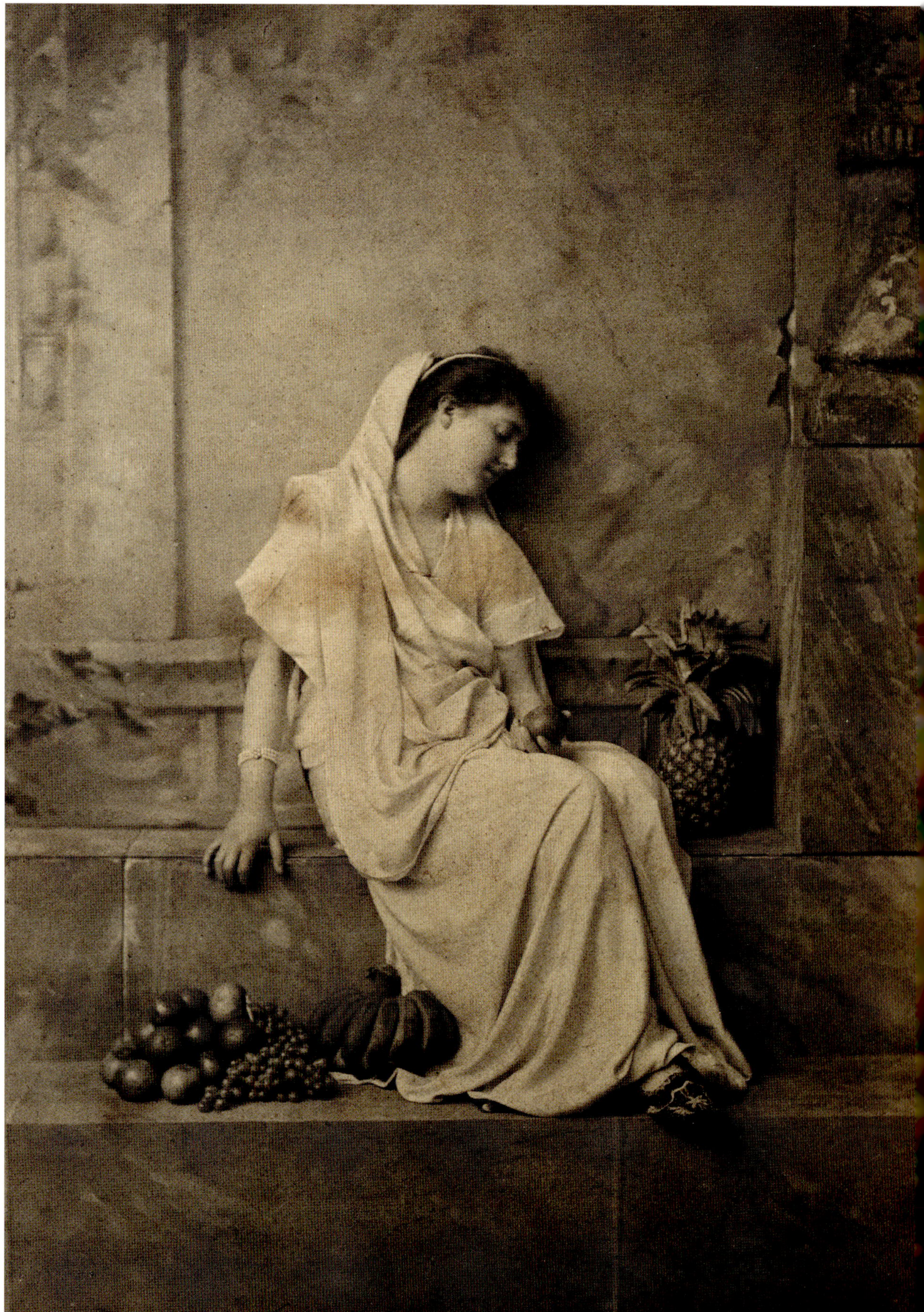

FIG. 36 | SHAPOOR N. BHEDWAR
*The Fair Fruitseller*
carbon print, 346 x 262 mm, c. 1890s, from *Art Studies* album
[ACP: 97.47.0001 (25)]

of Photography, entitled *Art Studies* (Fig. 36). He appears at a distinct moment in the history of photography in India, a world in which "artist-photographers" sought to merit their work based on the aesthetics of exchange between tradition, fine art and even performance. This allows a more complex and unrestrained view of the discipline, one in which the camera developed close links with painting and printmaking, a symbiotic relationship that transformed the ethics of engagement for perpetuity.

## Pre-studio photography in Bombay

The arrival of photography in India as early as 1840, eventually led to the establishment of the first photographic society in Bombay in 1854. The medium was primarily considered a means of documentation, and the government appointed two photographers to the Bombay Presidency, namely Thomas Biggs of the Bombay Artillery, and Dr. W.H. Pigou of the Bombay Medical Service.[2] It was felt that photography would achieve results with accuracy and speed, far better than any draughtsman could produce, and hence it was deployed for copying the antiquities of the areas surrounding Bombay, including the rendering of "historical and artistic" inscriptions.[3]

On the educational front, the Court of Directors of the East India Company recommended the patronage of photography, together with the provision of sufficient apparatus from England, to the Government of Bombay as early as 1845.[4] John Harkness, principal of the Elphinstone College addressed the issue in 1855, thus:

> "...those of have a taste for this useful art and are anxious to cultivate it, should have an opportunity of acquiring, from some skilful and experienced photographer, such a knowledge of the instruments and their various applications."[5]

Captain Barr, the president of Photographic Society of Bombay was asked for his suggestions and, in 1856, he agreed to the appointment of a "practical photographer" to take charge at the Elphinstone, as a provisional arrangement. In the meantime, Barr received an application from a W.H.S. Crawford for the job of photographic instructor at the Elphinstone. Another application received at this time was that of Dr. Narayen Dajee [Narayan Daji], who had graduated from Grant Medical College in 1852. Daji came supported with testimonials from his professors—Herbert Giraud, of chemistry and botony, and W.I. Coleston, of medical jurisprudence. Though the photographic department at the Elphinstone did not last for the years to come, the incentive to provide facilities for photography had entered the administration.[6]

With similar initiative for recording architectural sights and exploring the hinterland, the works of William Johnson, a civil servant, and William Henderson, a clerk, was actively commissioned as part of an ethnographic survey (also featured in the exhibition). Together, they published 24 issues of the *Indian Amateur's Photographic Album* (1856–1858), and contributed several

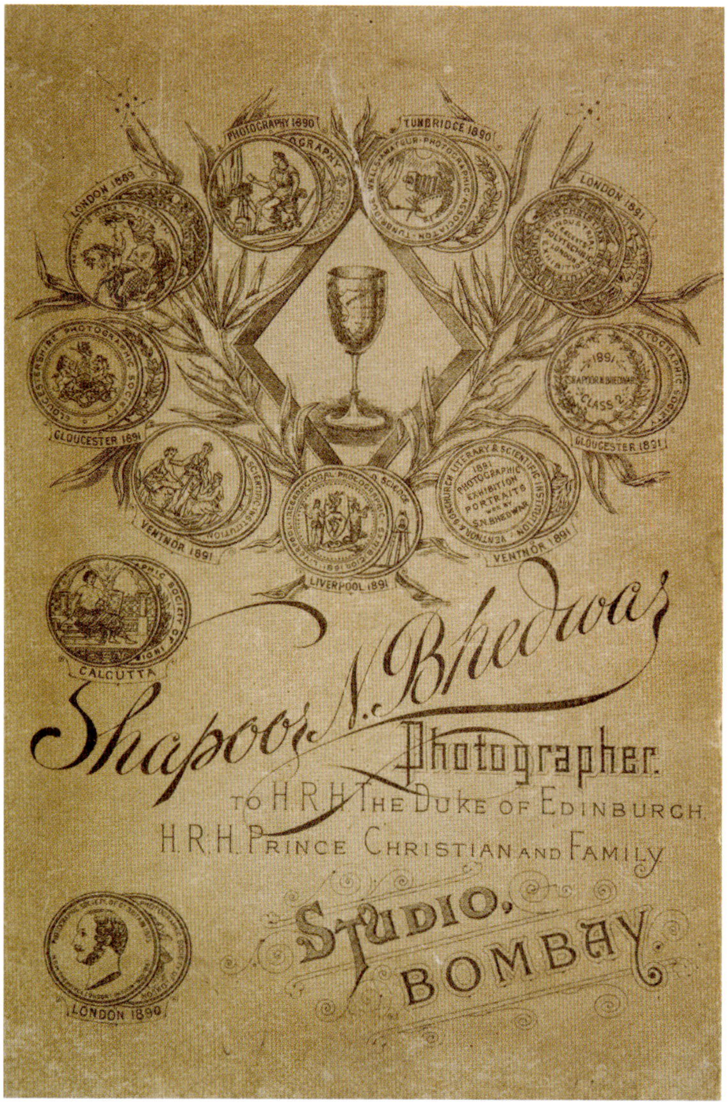


**FIG. 37 | SHAPOOR N. BHEDWAR**
Verso of Cabinet Card, 160 x 105mm, c. 1890s
[The Alkazi Collection of Photography]

photographs in published works ranging from "Costumes and Characters of Western India", *The Caves of Karla* (1861), and perhaps the most famous, *The Oriental Races and Tribes, Residents and Visitors of Bombay* published in two volumes in 1863 and 1866 respectively. Similar ventures were also highlighted by Sir Henry Hinton, schoolmaster and photographer in Bombay, who shot *Views of Beejapur* in the late 1850s, which were printed by Thomas Graham in 1860, in addition to the *Cave Temples of Ellora and Aurangabad*.[7]

The Bombay Government eventually established a committee of "Architectural Antiquities of Central India", chaired by H. Newton. In 1869, the government of Bombay continued its support for shooting the architectural remains to the architect James Burgess and the commercial photographer D.H. Sykes. However, by July 1870, the Archaeological Survey of India (ASI) was revived as the premier body to take photographs of the antiquities, with Alexander Cunningham as its president. Hence, the governments of the Bombay and Madras presidencies, which were responsible for the taking of photographs till now, gave the future authority to ASI.

Independent practitioners were on the rise by this time. Commercial studios had gradually been established, albeit by a majority of European photographers. They now shared experiences with their Indian counterparts, leading to a more expansive circulation and coverage of society at the time.[8] As an object, the coming of the family album or privately commissioned souvenir albums, together with card-mounted photographs, marked the democratization of the medium towards the end of the nineteenth century.

## Entering Bhedwar's studio

The relentless desire for creating a catalogue of India's monuments and broadening the study of its races and tribes, led to an opening of a new aesthetic of representation, through commissioned portraits in a format that closely corresponded with the painted miniature. The photographer had already entered the world of art exhibitions since the grand exhibition of 1851, including several subsequent expositions by the photographic societies in Calcutta, Bombay and Madras [now Chennai]. Here the medium shifted from the early daguerreotype, to the collodion positive, and ambrotypes, which were cheaper and quicker to produce.[9] Shapoor N. Bhedwar (b. 1858–c. 1915), based in Bombay, appeared at an opportune moment when independent studios

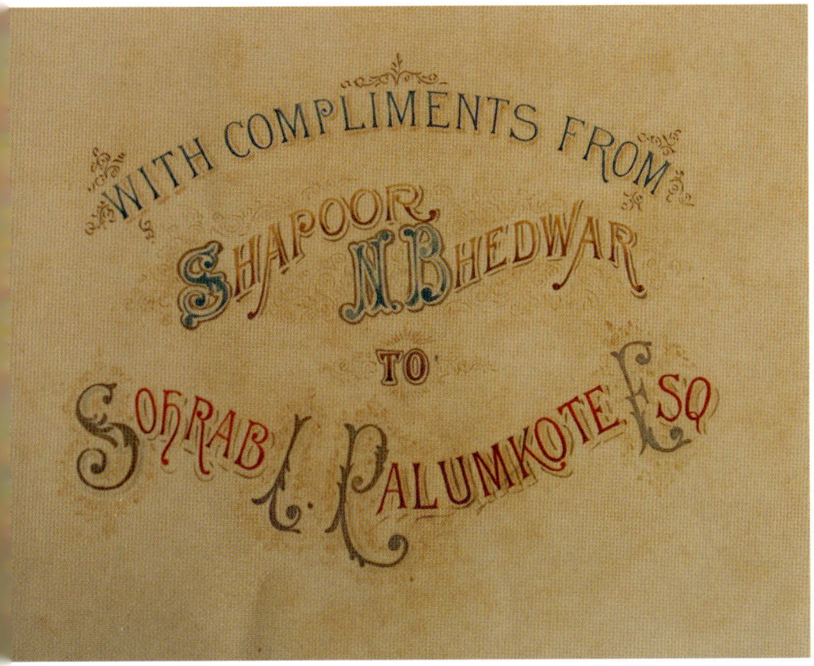


by resident photographers were on the rise and boldly expressing social desires through popular iconography. Furthermore, these photographers sought to publicise their spaces as art ateliers, equipped with statues, furniture and painted backdrops, and further conveyed by the versos of card-mounted photographs (Fig. 37).

The *Art Studies*, a "performance" album of 31 images, was compiled in c. 1890 in Bombay, but sections of it had very likely been produced in England. Bhedwar, who allegedly lived in Swiss Lodge, Cumballa Hill (an area preferred by the British and Parsis in the 1890s) was an extremely accomplished photographer.[10] Additionally, he was an affiliate member of the Scottish Freemasonry Lodge. He travelled to London in 1889 to study photography, where his work later received several gold medals, including the exhibitions in Liverpool and the Royal Photographic Society "salons" in London (between 1891 and 1893). In England, he was a friend of Ward Muir, a critic and writer for the British photographic press as well as the art-photographer Ralph W. Robinson, son of the pioneer Pictorialist photographer H.P. Robinson. The allegorical style of Robinson was echoed in Bhedwar's two narrative series "The Feast of Roses" and "The Initiation of a Zoroastrian Priest" (a few of the latter possibly appear towards the end of the narrative series called "Renunciation Series" by Bhedwar in *Art Studies*), certain plates of which were also reproduced in *The Illustrated London News* with a text by the renowned travelling painter in India, William Simpson (1823–1899).[11]

FIG. 38 | UNKNOWN ARTIST, POSSIBLY SHAPOOR N. BHEDWAR
*Art Studies*, Album Inner Title Page, watercolour and ink, c. 1890s
[ACP: 97.47.0001]

The first page of the album identifies the patron and the photographer, both of whose status appear to be equally important, the former identified by the name, Sohrab Palamkote (Fig. 38). He was a patron of the arts, a Gujarati poet, after whom a hall was also named in the Dadar area of Mumbai. The album itself is divided into distinct sections, and is perhaps one of the first Indo-European theatrical stylizations in photography. It flows as a compilation of images of both communities, instructed in manners, gestures and stereotypical poses, followed by a staged performance piece in photographic form.

The image entitled *"Gool Guli–A Rose Bud"* was the first in this compelling series for the patron (Fig. 39). Seductively posed, this image of a lady from the Orient clearly falls within the iconography of a romantic paradigm. The aristocratic space engulfs her in the flamboyant message of self-proclamation, as though to communicate that behind the curtains of a boudoir, lies an object of complete and unrelenting desire. However, the image also brings forth a kind of visuality quite different from those of female royalty at the time, and more in keeping with a "courtesans' art". Unlike women who were depicted in *purdah*, veiled from the eye and socially secluded, the role

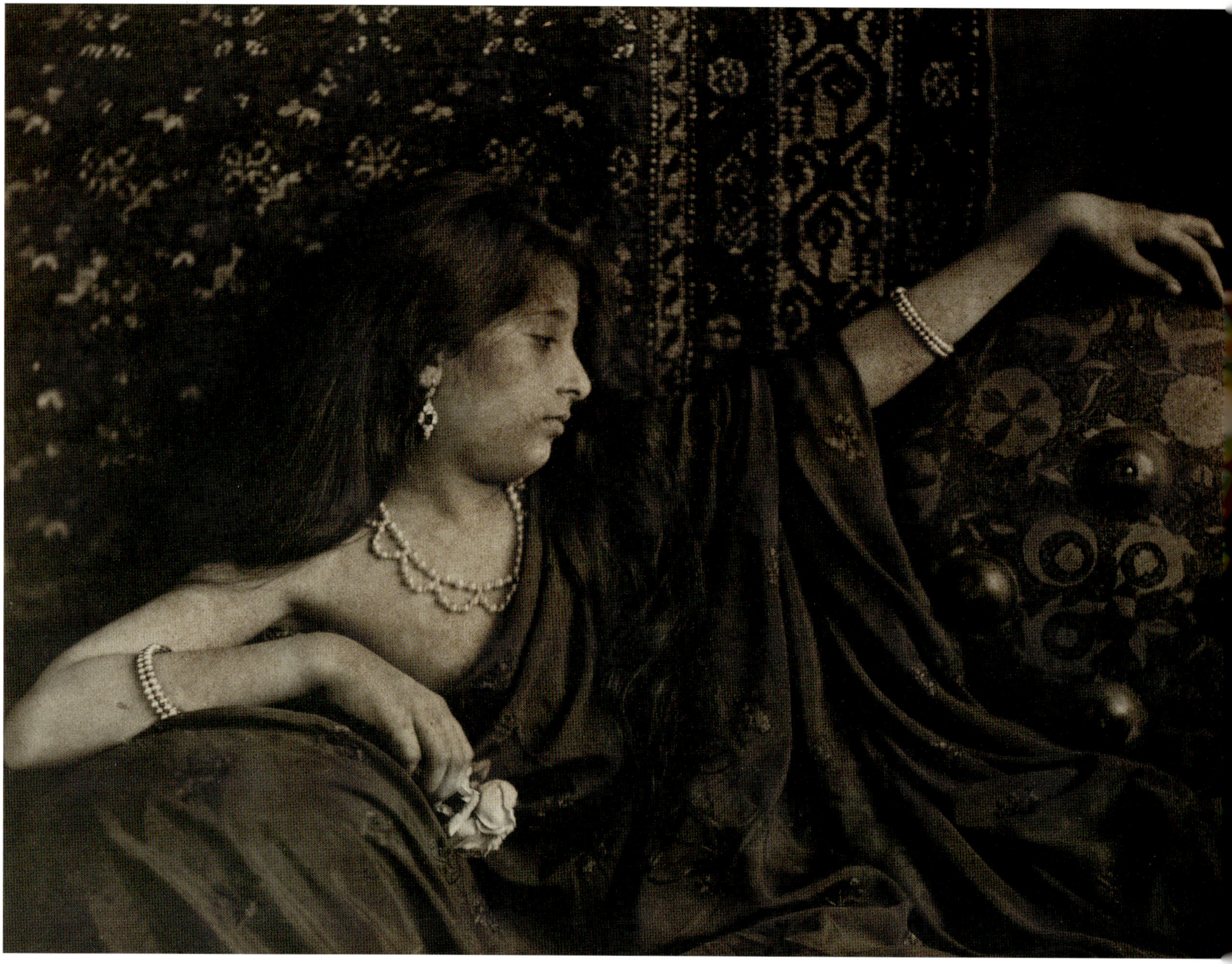

FIG. 39 | SHAPOOR N. BHEDWAR
*Gool Guli—A Rose Bud*
carbon print, 275 x 362 mm, c. 1890s,
from *Art Studies* album [ACP: 97.47.0001 (01)]

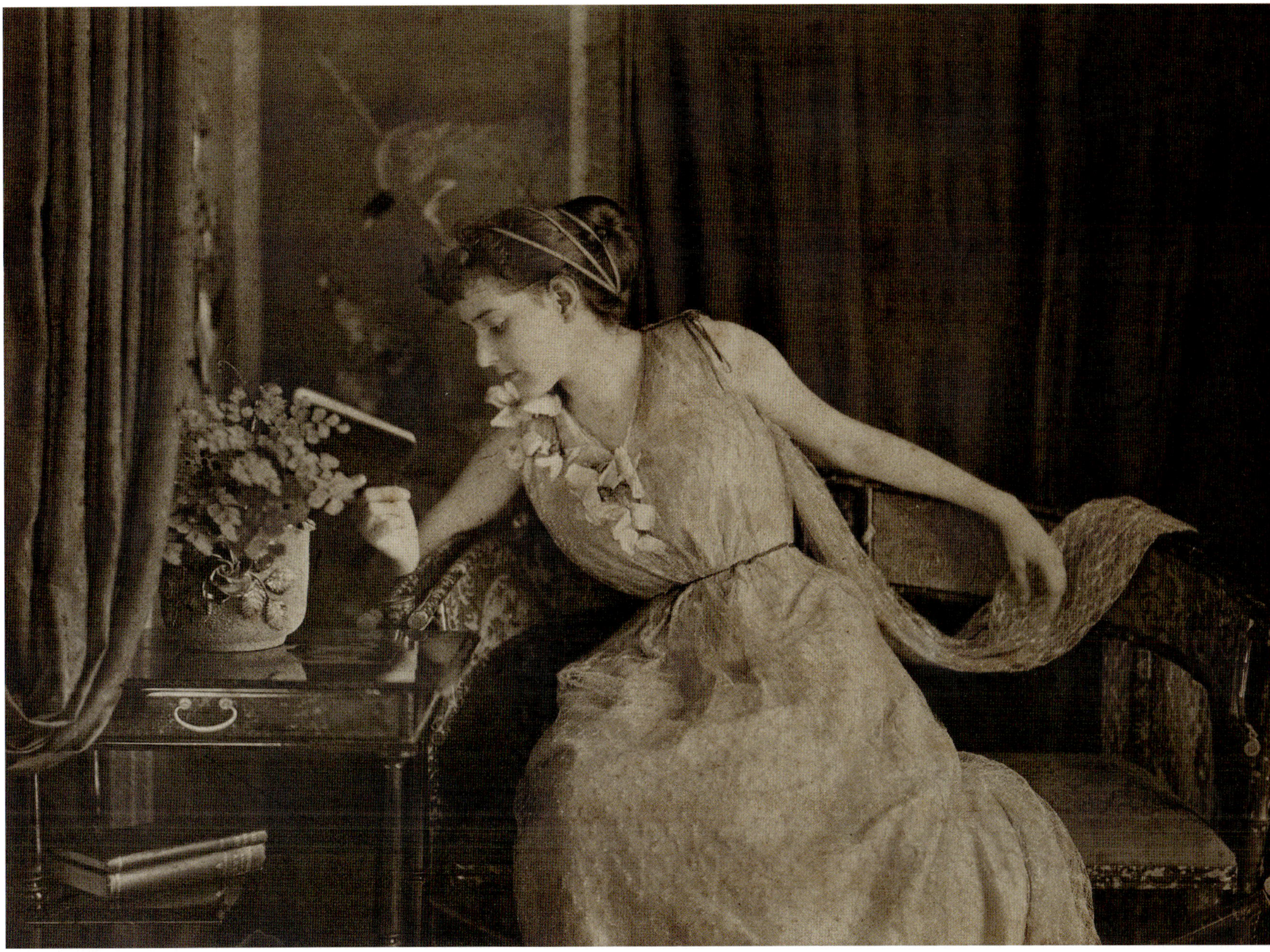

FIG. 40 | SHAPOOR N. BHEDWAR
*A Page from Shelly*
carbon print, 268 x 344 mm, c. 1890s,
from *Art Studies* album [ACP: 97.47.0001 (02)]

of a courtesan was to address the public, and embrace the unrestricted exposure to their clients. Such a sense is even conveyed in the images of the Lucknow album, *Beauties of Lucknow* (1855), by Darogha Abbas Ali, mentioned earlier in this volume by Prof. Mitter.

The second image in this series is entitled *"A Page from Shelley"* (Fig. 40), representing a Victorian lady engrossed in a book. These leisurely activities continue throughout the album, but speculation with the Indian lady depicted before posits a curious hypothesis. A learned European woman immediately follows the seductive Asian lady. This is not an incidental or inconsequential arrangement, but one that clearly provokes an internal discourse on gender, delineated by race in the East and West. This is conceivably an attempt at moulding the sensual female into a woman of character in order to bridge the two introductory images. But despite Bhedwar's intentions, they also create infractions that broaden the gap in the role of women in the nineteenth century: between the world of the wife and that of the courtesan.

The next set of extraordinary images comes under the larger banner of "The Feast of Roses", a series that won awards in London and Cardiff in the 1890s. Here, European women come together, as the *Flower Girl, Heaving the Garland, Confidences, Inamurata* or the female lover as it translates from Italian and eventually the *Messenger* (Fig. 41). They are images associated with innocence, while simultaneously articulating a distinct connection with high Victorian fine art, and they were perhaps a set of images used for conceptualising a group of oil paintings.

A reference to the painter Raja Ravi Varma in this context is important for two reasons: first, he enabled people from all over the country to look at identical images being produced by his press (established in 1892, with machinery from Germany). Furthermore because of his leaning towards Western mannerism and his selection of Indian subjects and themes, his images became local interpretations of national themes in a hybrid visual format. Varma's style matured through his attempt of internalizing and expressing the subtleties of European art, geometric perspective and the objective rendering from photographs.[12]

Some of his images are highly reminiscent of the "The Feast of Roses" series, representing traditional roles of females, seen in compositions such as *Manorama* and *Malyala Sundari* (1890s). The emphasis laid on the female figure in these studies goes a step beyond his mythological work, just like Bhedwar's work doesn't merely fulfill a European fantasy. While religion serves as a backdrop for Varma, his paintings of a Malabar or Parsi beauty, also communicate moods ranging from bashfulness to feigned arrogance, similar to the sentiments communicated by Bhedwar's studies.

FIG. 41 | SHAPOOR N. BHEDWAR
*The Feast of Roses—Heaving the Garland*
carbon print, 267 x 354 mm, c. 1890s,
from *Art Studies* album [ACP: 97.47.0001 (07)]

## Pictorialism and The Renunciation Series

It is important to mention here that Bhedwar was one of the earliest exponents of the Pictorialist style in photography, arising from movements of the *fin-de-siécle*, represented by

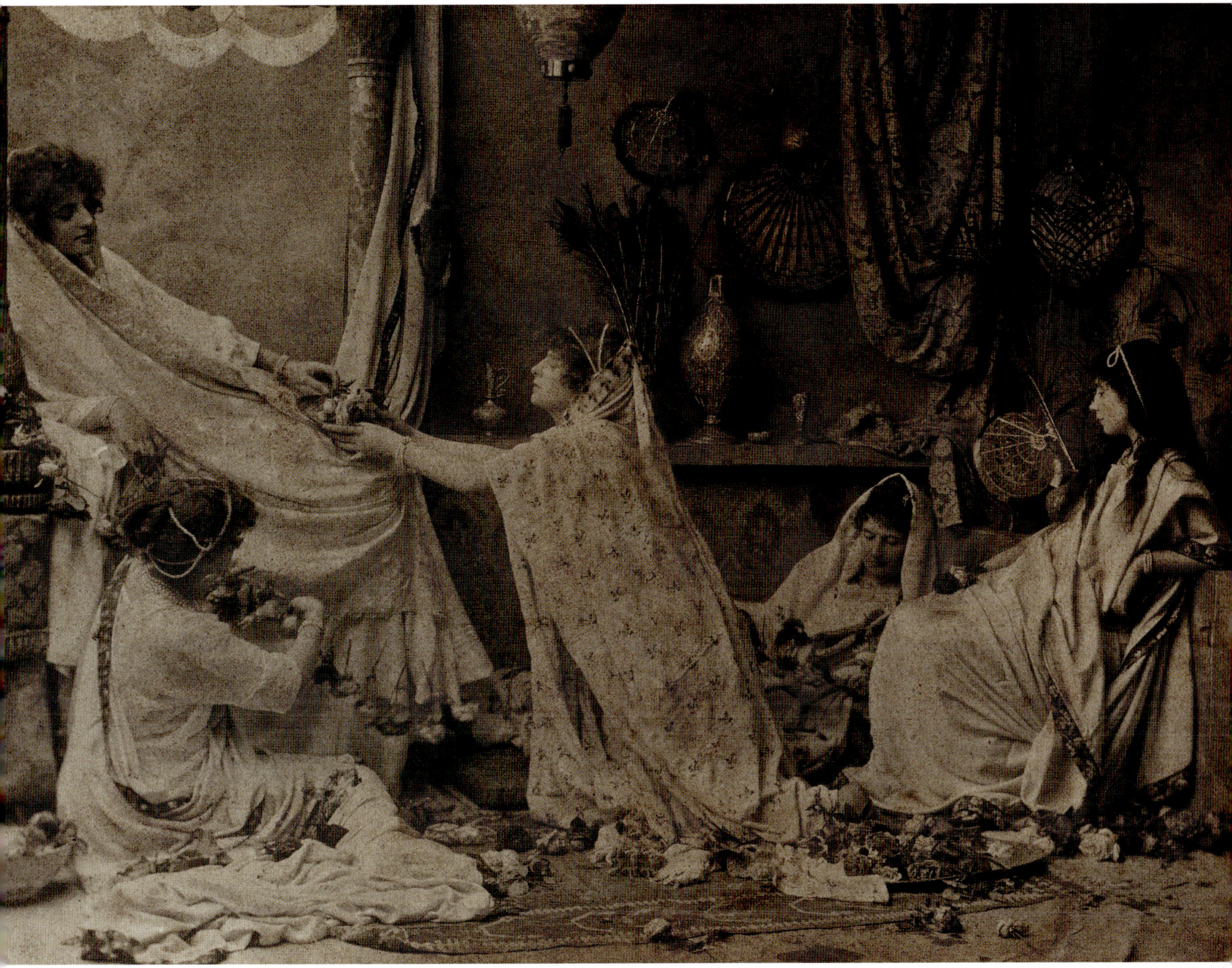

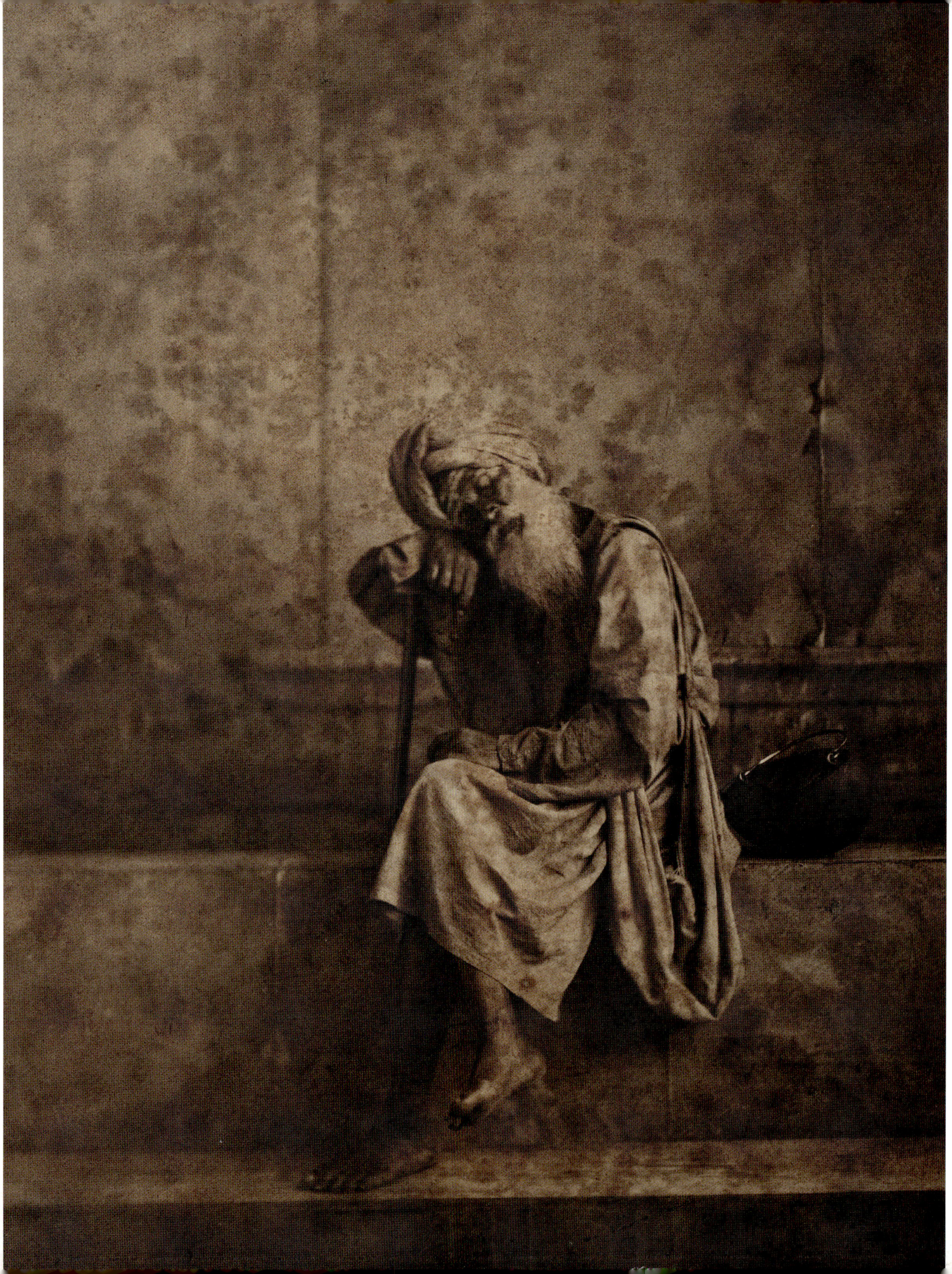

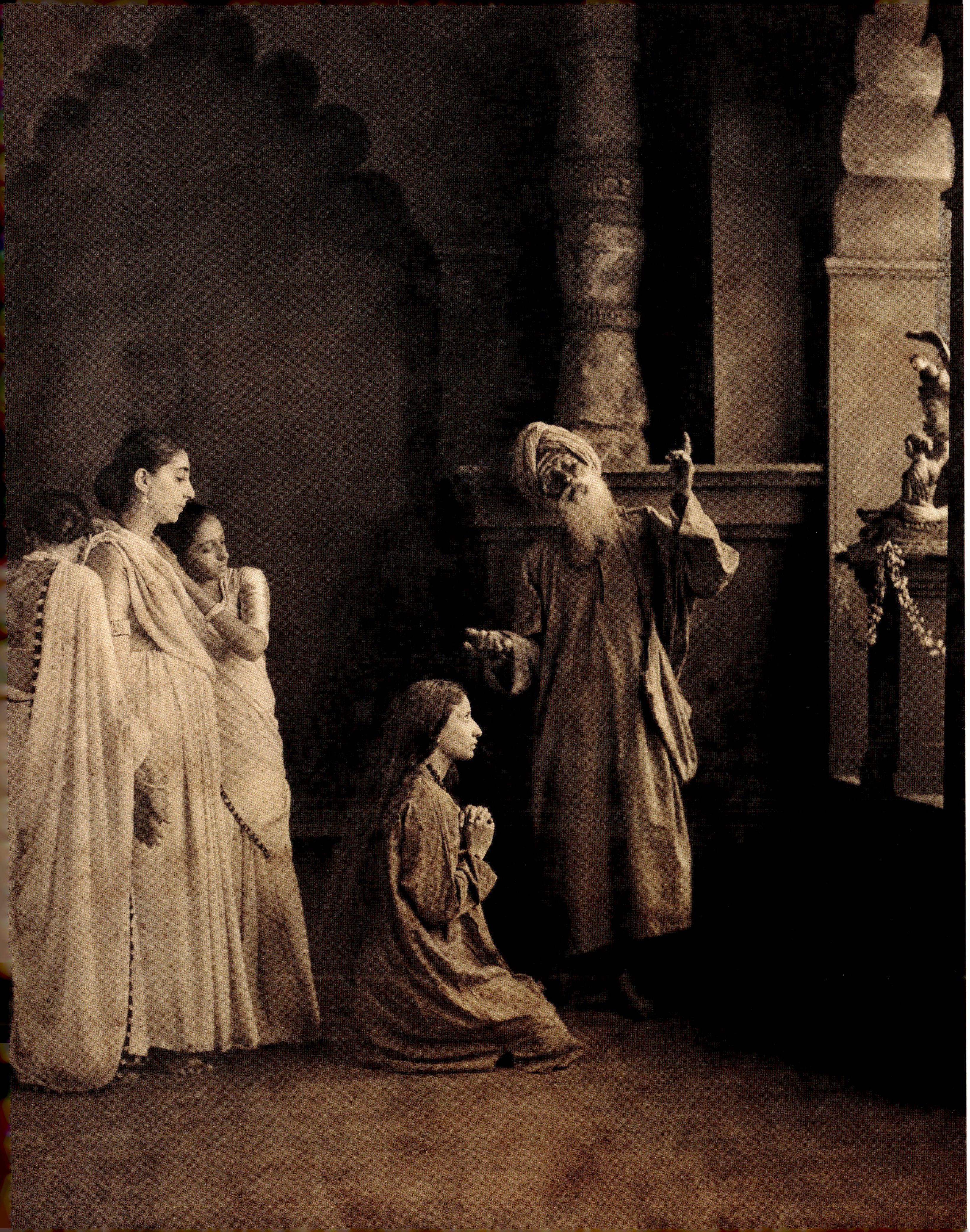

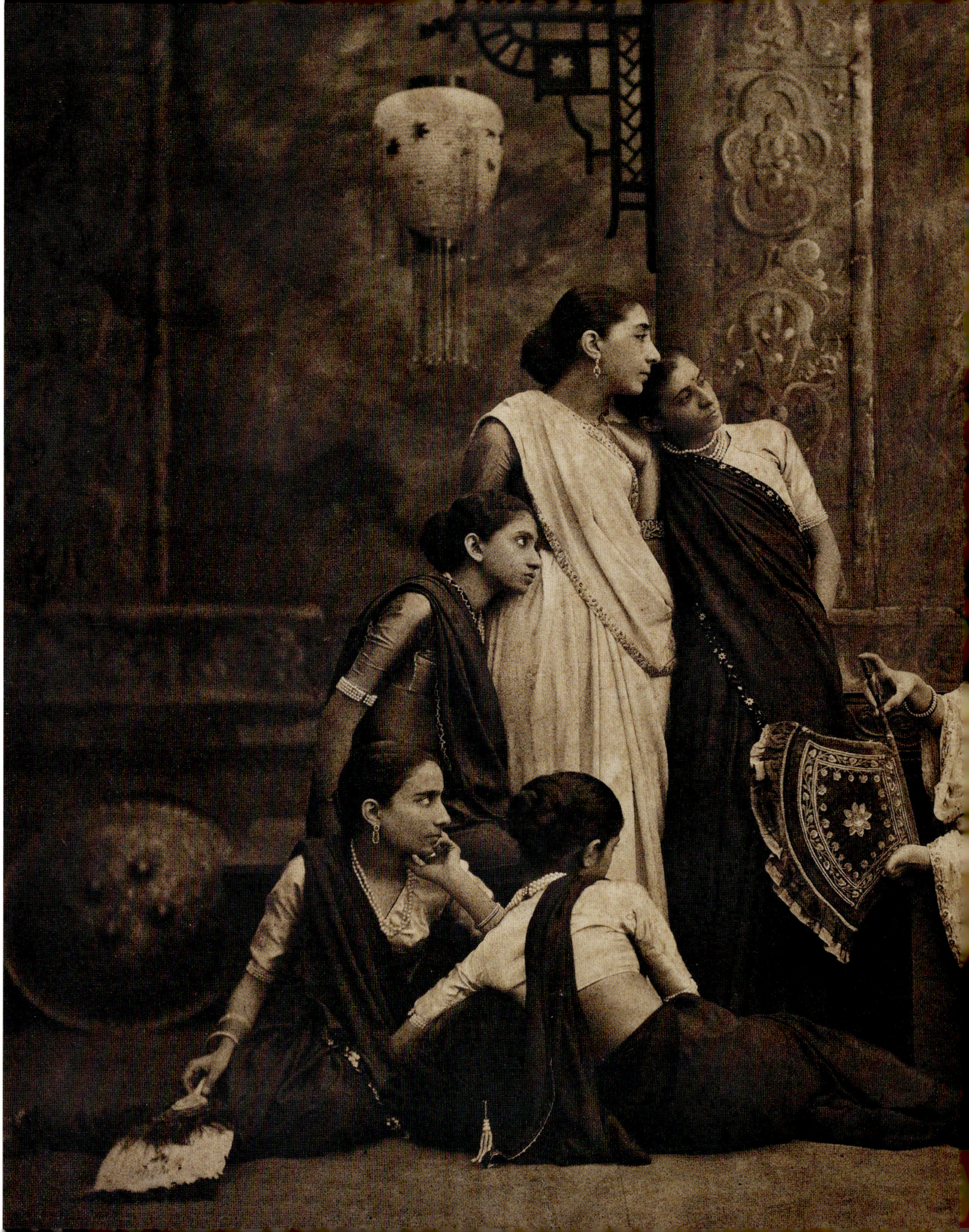

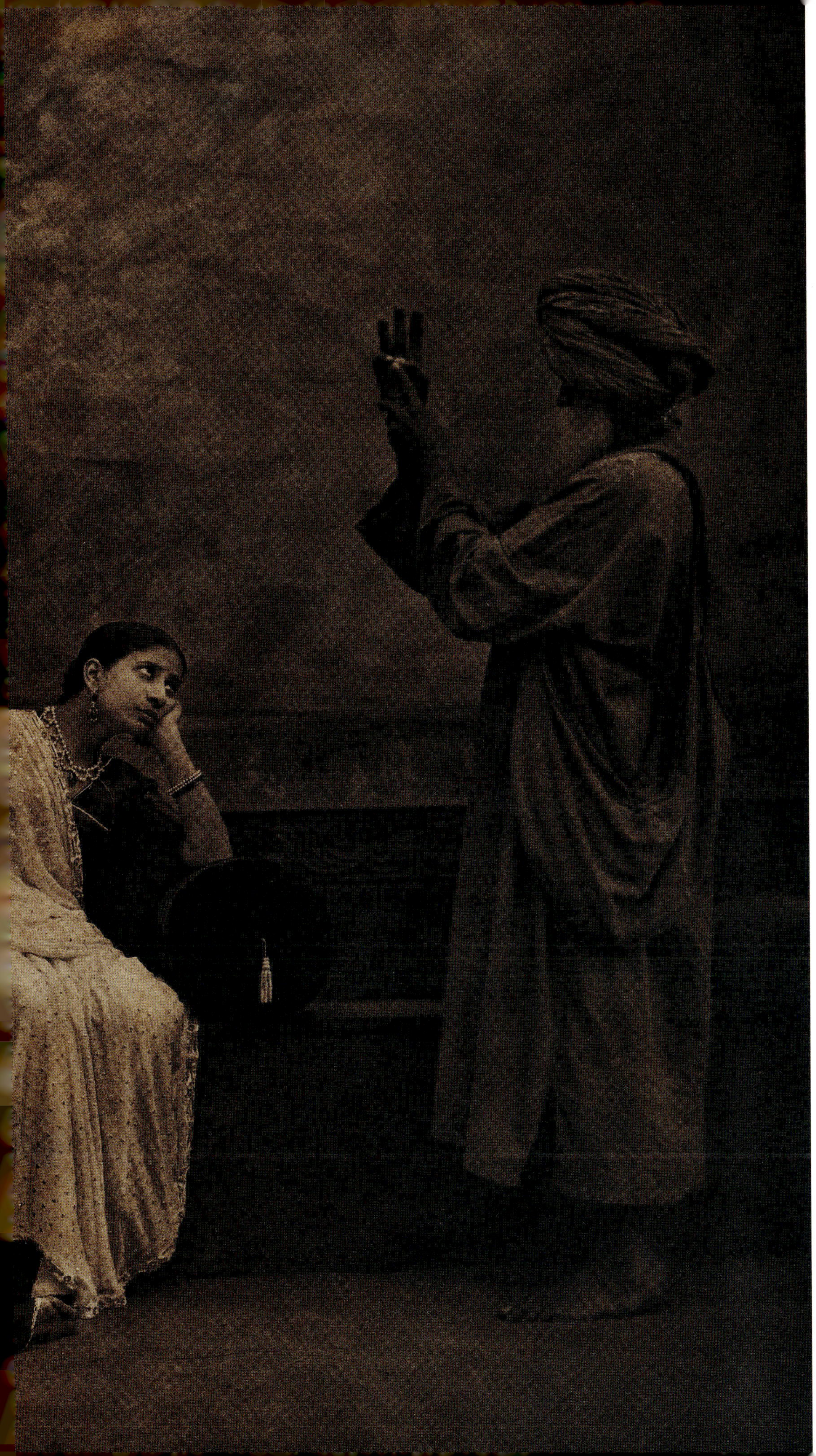

PAGE 66

FIG. 42 | SHAPOOR N. BHEDWAR
*Tyag No. 1 – Weary sits the Yogi-Raj*
carbon print, 340 x 254 mm, c. 1890s,
from *Art Studies* album [ACP: 97.47.0001 (12)]

PAGE 67

FIG. 43 | SHAPOOR N. BHEDWAR
*Tyag No. 6 – The World Renounced*
carbon print, 338 x 273 mm, c. 1890,
from *Art Studies* album [ACP: 97.47.0001 (17)]

FIG. 44 | SHAPOOR N. BHEDWAR
*Tyag No. 4 – The Mystic Sign*
carbon print, 260 x 345 mm, c. 1890s,
from *Art Studies* album [ACP: 97.47.0001 (15)]

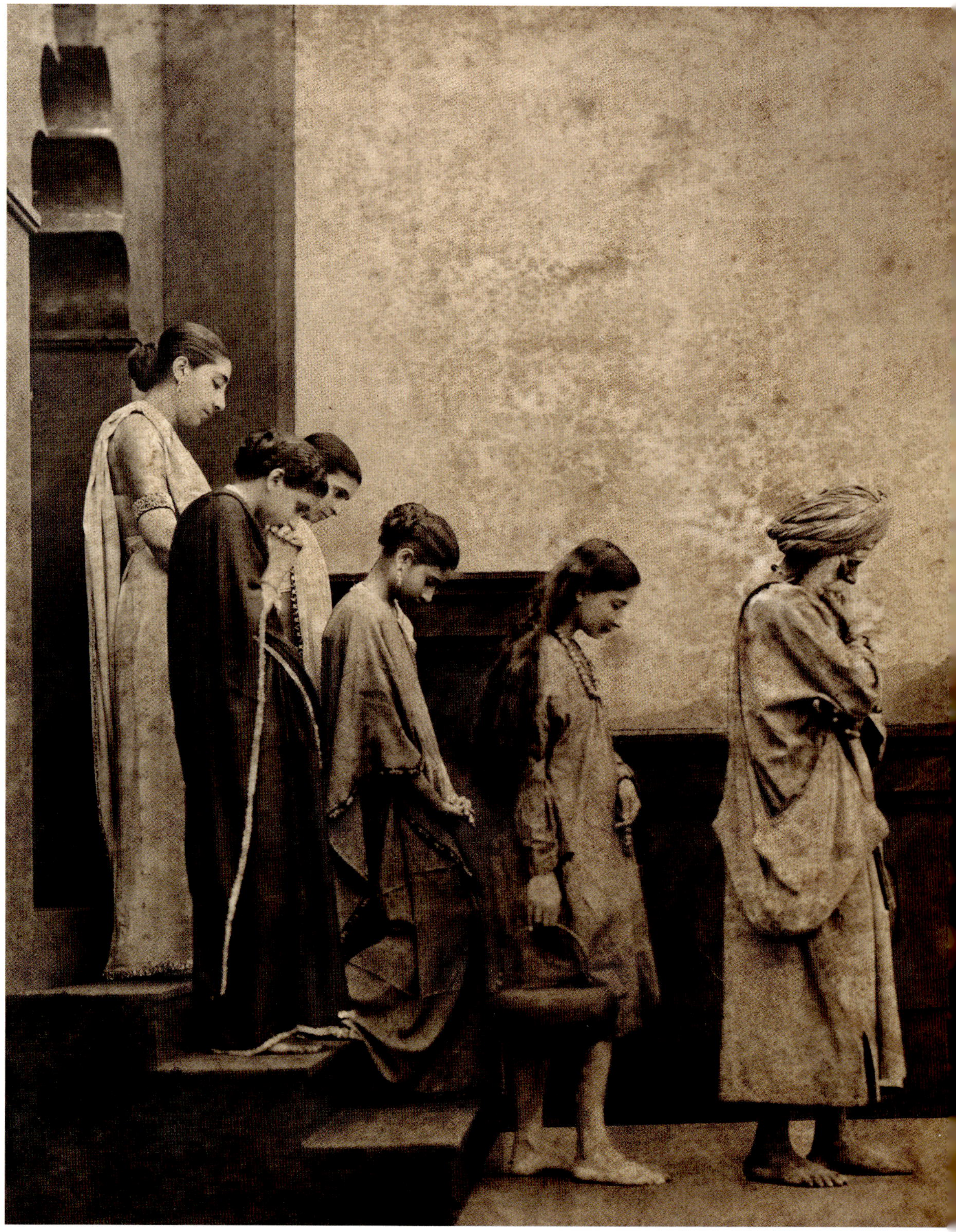

FIG. 45 | SHAPOOR N. BHEDWAR
*Tyag No. 8 – On the Temple Step*
carbon print, 338 x 273 mm, c. 1890s,
from *Art Studies* album [ACP: 97.47.0001 (19)]

atmospheric compositions and lyrical modes. His European counterparts would have included photographers such as Alexander Keighley, Paul Bergon and Frederick Henry Evans, all of whom, like Bhedwar, produced photogravure work.[13]

Bhedwar began, on one of his trips to England, to participate in the activities of a creative group who called themselves the Brotherhood of the Linked Ring that was founded in April 1892, having broken away from London's Royal Photographic Society. The members of the Linked Ring were dedicated to "art photography", reacting against industrialization in general and the ease of the instantaneous "snapshot". Bhedwar and his colleagues sought to produce work that consciously drew on the conventions of painting, emphasizing the photographer as an artist. They constructed compositions that were often inspired by allegorical or mythical subject matter, much like Ravi Varma. Bhedwar eventually won a number of medals in England and Indian salons and published some images in 1893 in the American journal Camera Notes, edited by Alfred Stieglitz.[14] The latter also initiated a similar photography movement called "Photo-Secession Movement" in 1902 that was in existence till 1917.

The last portion of the album is perhaps the most intriguing of all, entitled "The Renunciation Series" (Fig. 42). It is the story of a yogi, composed perhaps even as an actual theatrical performance in the Elphinstone or the Ripon. As the yogi, named Raj, comes upon a house of very attractive and idle women, he seems to completely capture their imaginations, and fuel their desires, their vapid empty lives, with a spiritual quest, to renounce the world of tactile, composite objects in search of meaning (Figs 43–44). It is the story of a man who carefully and selectively suggests how men/women can exist in a world that is not a material one, but rather a sensory experience driven by beliefs. The women eventually follow him from the Palladian domains in a well-balanced and dramatic image (Fig. 45).

The theme of the series also resonates that of the historical yogi Gopichandra. In medieval Indian history, he was the son of Raja Trilok Chandra of Bengal and became a disciple of Jalandhara Nath leaving his kingdom at the insistence of his mother, Mayanamati. She gave him long speeches on the vanity of the world, its possessions and the necessity of a spiritual existence. The story of Gopichandra's renunciation has become classical, and Ravi Varma also painted it for mass dissemination through his press.[15]

Was this performance one that renounced high Victorian culture, or was this a kind of theatre, with painted backdrops and theatrical props, a medium that could bind people to a tradition? Was this album a step towards the emancipation of women through a popular medium, or did Pictorialism as an artistic movement represent mere sentimentality? Bhedwar, to my mind, manages to fill a very important vacuum through his dramatized visual lexicon and carefully selected themes (European and Indian), namely, the evolution of a new visuality premised on the ethics of cultural-fusion.

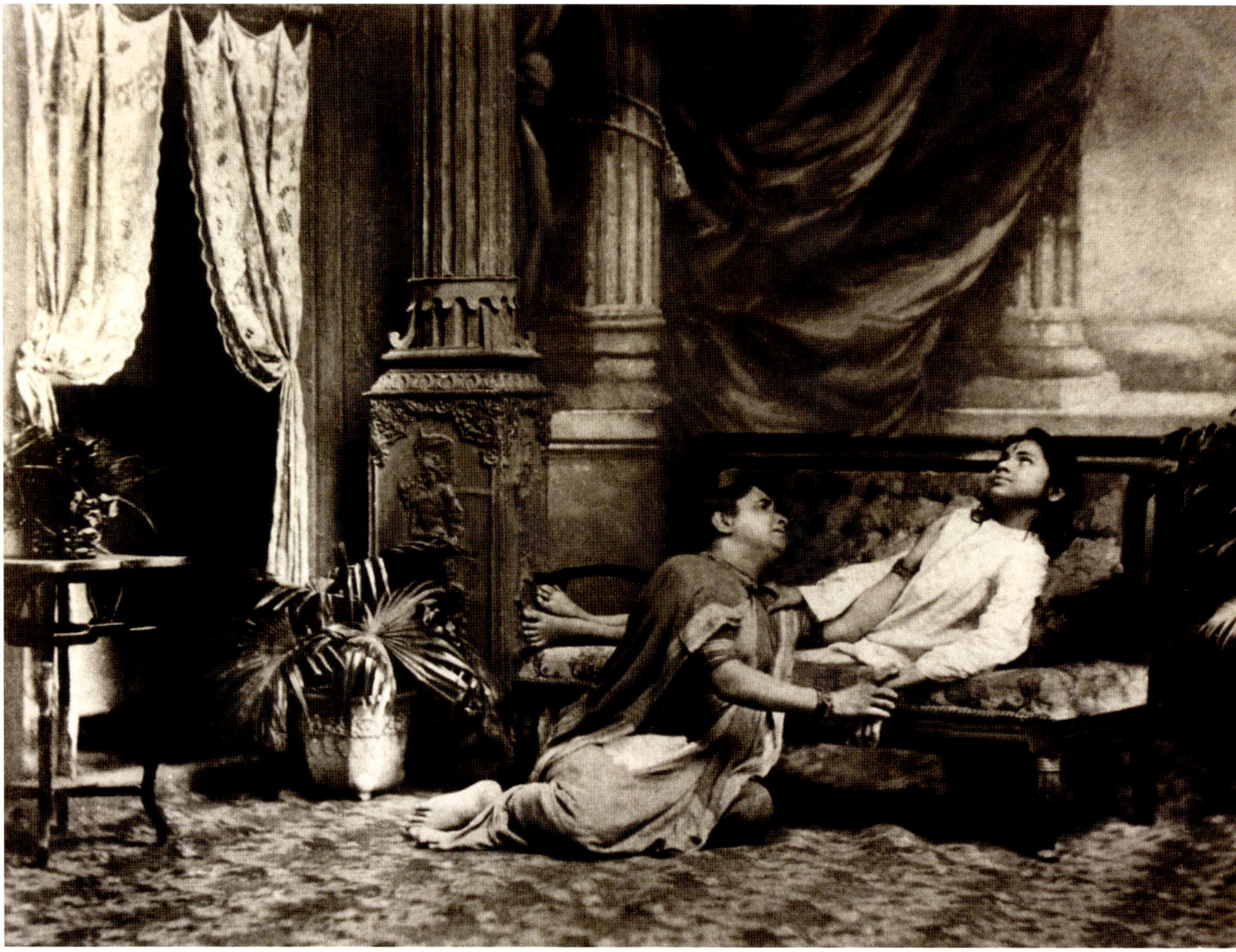

FIG. 46 | UNKNOWN PHOTOGRAPHER
Performance of a play titled *"Satwapariksha"* in Nagpur by the Maharashtrian Natak Mandali
gelatin silver print, 1915
[Courtesy: Nissar Allana Collection]

The yogi represents the epitome of a noble savage, rescuing those corrupted by idleness and the "fatigue of the modern". Such social awareness was also the impulse that created the Marathi Natya Sangeet and innumerable Parsi *natak* groups, avidly documented by studios in Bombay such as the Rex[16] (Fig. 46). And so, a careful inversion of power was fulfilled through the very same medium that was allegedly propagating power for Europe in India, the camera.

In conclusion, Bhedwar's album is much like a scrapbook of expressions that creates a narrative on the history of representation and transition between painting and photography. The images veer between the interlinked domains of reality and drama, and here we find the alluring idea and function of "stillness"—temporal and spatial stillness—which becomes the canvas of captured performances and portraits. However, Bhedwar exists in the world of the growing number of studios such as EOS, the Bombay Photographic Society, Lala Deen Dayal & Sons, and S. Hormusji, among several others that provide fresh nourishment for photography as an indomitable modern art practice.

*Note: I would like to thank Ms. Gael Newton, Senior Curator of Australian and International Photography, National Gallery of Modern Art, Australia, for sharing aspects of her research, together with Deepti Mulgund, research assistant at the Dr. Bhau Daji Lad Museum.*

NOTES

1 John Hannavy, "The Daguerreotype Studio", in *Victorian Photographers at Work* (Princes Risborough: Shire Books, 1997), 24.

2 Janet Dewan, "Delineating Antiquities and Remarkable Tribes—Photography for Bombay and Madras Governments, 1855–70", *History of Photography Journal* 16, no. 4 (winter 1992): 302

3 Paraphrase of the *India and Bengal Despatch*, no. 22 (7 February, 1855) IOR.

4 Ray Desmond, *India office Library and Records Report* (1974), 37.

5 G. Thomas, "Photography and the Elphinstone Institution of Bombay," in *History of Photography: An International Quarterly* 5, no. 3 (July 1981): 245.

6 *ibid.*, p. 246.

7 The Photographic Collector 5, no. 1 (Spring 1984), 19–21. For further details on ethnographic studies in India see John Falconer, "Ethnographical Photography in India—1850–1900", *Photographic Collector* 5, no. 1 (1984):16–46; Christopher Pinney, "Colonial Anthropology in the Laboratory of Mankind", in *An Illustrated History of India*, ed. C.A.Bayly (New Delhi: Oxford University Press, 1991).

8 Janet Dewan, "Delineating Antiquities and Remarkable Tribes: Photography for Bombay and Madras Governments, 1855–70," *History of Photography* Journal 16, no. 4 (winter 1992): 315.

9 John Falconer and Louise Hide, *Points of View: Capturing the 19th Century in Photographs* (London: British Library Publishing, 2009), 16–17.

10 http://erps.dmu.ac.uk/catalogue_single.php?h=ca2&pnum=E94A007&page=p&efn=Shapoor+N.+Bhedwar (accessed on 29.01.2010).

11 Margaret Harker, *The Linked Ring: The Secession Movement in Photography in Britain—1892–1910*, Royal Photographic Society Publication, (London: Heinemann, 1979), 147.

12 Castelli Enrico and Aprile Giovanni, *Divine Lithography* (New Delhi: Eastern Book Corporation, 2005), 98.

13 John Falconer and Louise Hide, *Points of View: Capturing the 19th Century in Photographs* (London: British Library Publishing, 2009) 162–167.

14 Ian Jeffery, *How to Read a Photograph: Understanding, Interpreting and Enjoying the Great Photographers* (London: Thames and Hudson, 2008), 28. See: http://www.thefreelibrary.com/The+colonial+project+and+the+shifting+gaze.-a0182035429 (accessed on 29.01.2010).

15 Castelli Enrico and Aprile Giovanni, *Divine Lithography* (New Delhi: Eastern Book Corporation, 2005), 66.

16 Nissar Allana, *Introduction to Painted Sceneries: Backdrops of the 19th century Marathi Natya Sangeet* (New Delhi: Theatre and Television Associates, 2008).

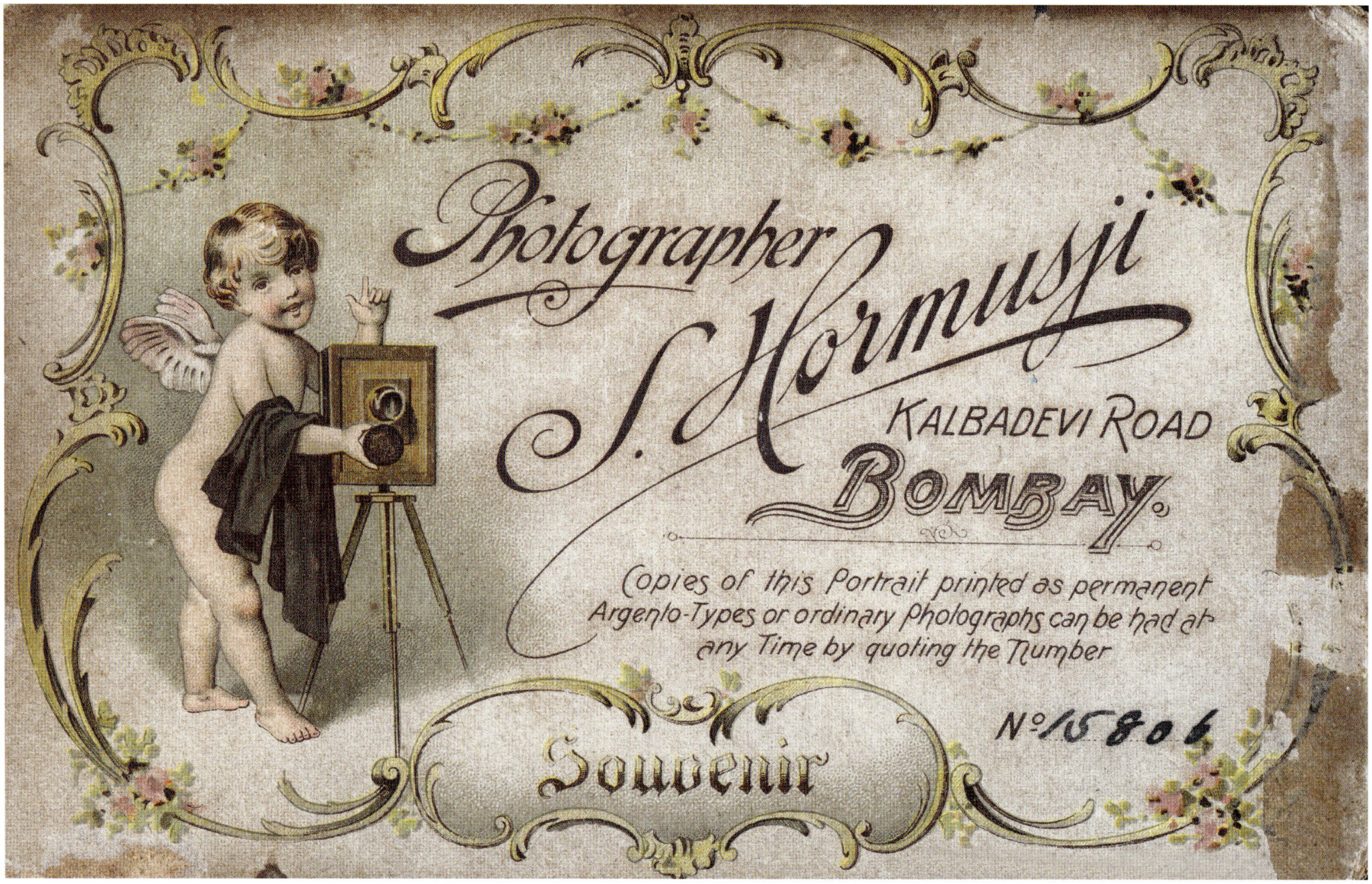


**Fig. i | S. HORMUSJI, BOMBAY**
Verso of Cabinet Card, 164 x 106 mm,
c. 1880–1890s
Photographer's Ref. 15806
[ACP: D2003.05.0048]

# FROM BOMBAY TO MUMBAI
## Studios of the City

Rahaab Allana

A cursory glance at the mounts and versos of innumerable photographs from the late-nineteenth century in Mumbai reveal exciting aesthetic and sociological traces of the city's cultural history. A majority of the studios were located in the Fort area, Merewether Street or on Kalbadevi Road—locales that catered to a growing middle class at the time. Among the popular studios were: P. Gomes & Co., P. Vuccino & Co., S. Hormusji, National Photo Co. (fig. i), Fred a Lair and innumerable others. These studios expedited their sales by advertising along artistic lines with a clear connection to a pictorial tradition, more so of the Victorian era, rather than merely being studios patronised for straightforward documentation.

One of the early studios that still exists is Indian Art Studio (fig. ii), or Premiere Palace, founded in 1917, located on Princess Street, as it was once known, now functioning under proprietor

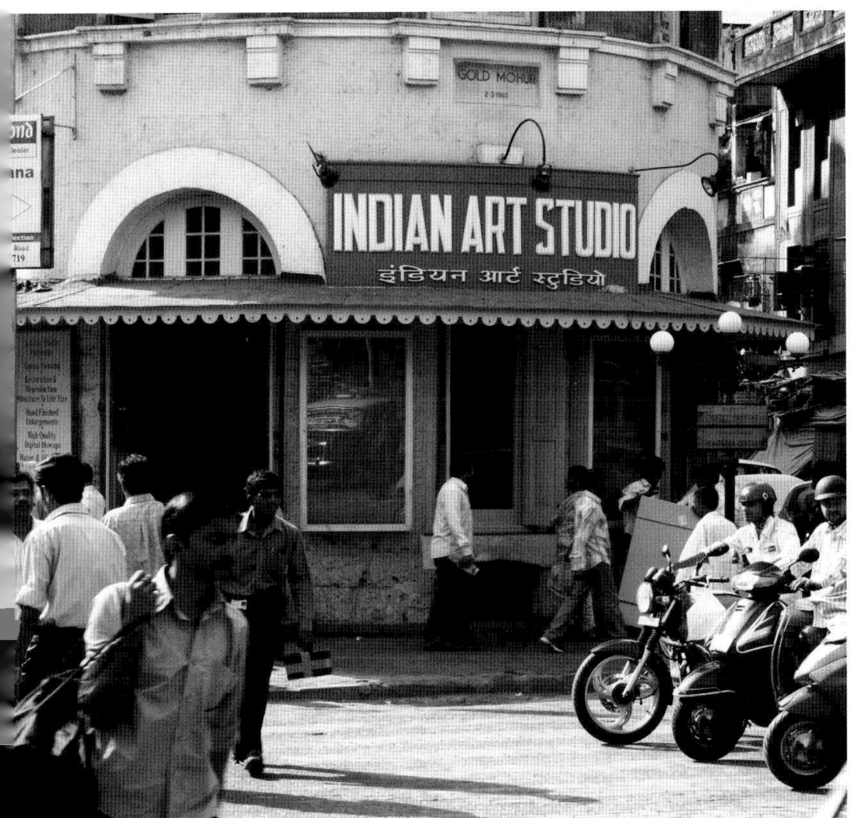


**Fig. ii** | The exterior of **Indian Art Studio**, founded in 1917. Photo: Manoj Pandey, 2009

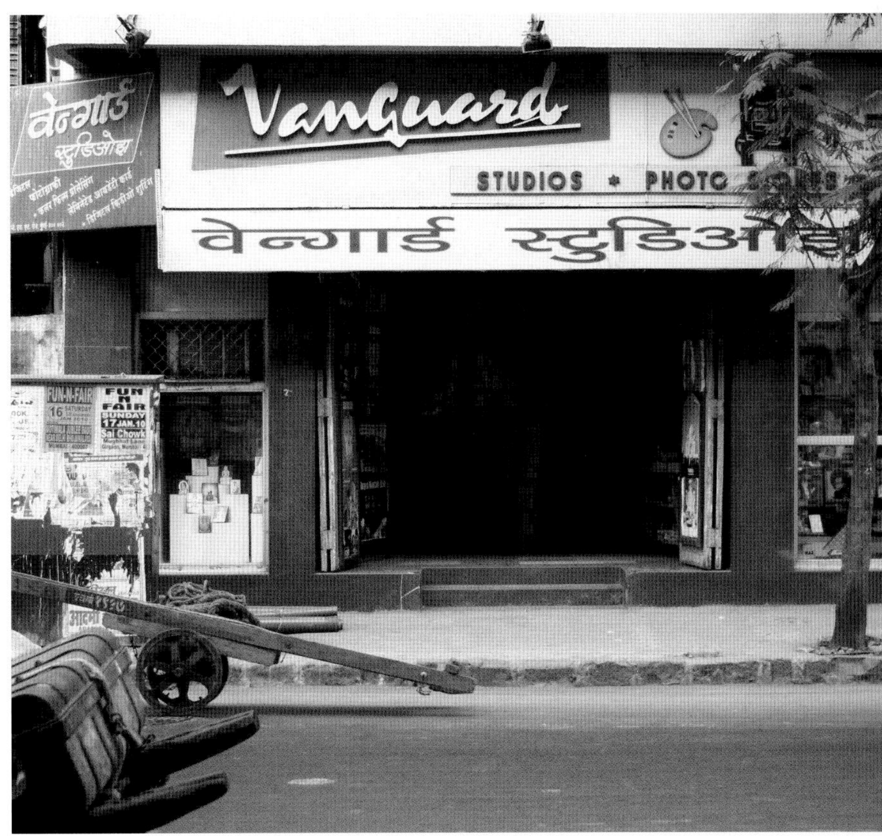


**Fig. iii** | **Vanguard Studio** established in 1927, allegedly the oldest studio in Girgaum. Photo: Manoj Pandey, 2009

Rajesh Chaddha. Upon entering the grand space, one is confronted by painted photographs and images of yesteryears[1]. Chaddha is keen to develop a part of the studio's basement area into a gallery for the studio's early photographs.

Another studio in the vicinity is Vanguard Studio (fig. iii), established in 1927 on J.S.S. Road. Now managed by Mahendra Sanghvi and his elder brother Harshavadanbhai, it is allegedly the oldest studio in the Girgaum area, and where many political leaders from the Independence movement posed, including Subhash Chandra Bose.[2] Studios like these are therefore important reminders of a bygone era of photography in India, as many have perished with the coming of new technologies in the digital age. Luckily, several older studios can still be identified by the lithographic versos on card-mounted images. These versos indicate a growing network of the circulation of photographs in India, on a national and even international scale.

P. VUCCINO & CO., BOMBAY
Verso of Cabinet Card, 163 x 105 mm, c. 1870–1890s [ACP: D2008.01.0019]

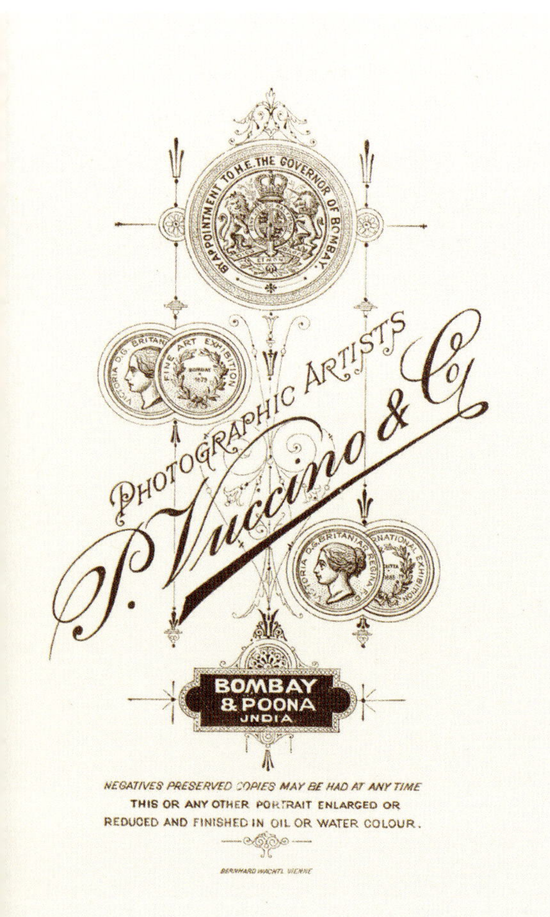


## Verso Culture

Marion & Co. from Paris was an important business that worked with photographic studios in India for the production of card-mounted photographs with lithographic inscriptions. They also developed a trade list, catalogues listing titles and inviting mail orders, employing photographers, purchasing negatives, and even copying the images that seemed marketable. Often a company would buy prints of prominent noblemen, re-photograph them, and sell them again.[3] There was a kind of "cartomania", in which the small format became a type of photographic literacy for the world and for Indian images to disseminate internationally. It indicated a revolution in print media, as studios in India started liaising with Marion quite early on. These included Bourne & Shepherd, Sachè & Westfield, Sachè & Murray, Lindley & Warren, Harichand Chintamon etc.

The coming of photographic democratization, or mass dissemination and usage, is therefore suggested by cards with printed frames called cartouche, usually in gilt or black. They became more elaborate with time and by the 1870s photographers offered their customers a choice of several styles of mounts at varying different prices. The photographer's identification appears as a logo, identical images mounted on cards with different typographies represents printing at different times. Blind stamps were also used with names and addresses placed on the face of a mount. The stamps themselves present the photographer's name, partnerships, slogans, gallery names, services offered by the studio, price schedules, styles and portraits.[4]

Often, a specific manner of lighting and shading was used by photographers to augment specific facial features. There were various kinds of effects that were utilized to even draw a connection with erstwhile painters and the brush effects they made. Knowledge of the techniques of the master painters was part of the formal training in art and thus became part of the studio photographer's stylistic lexicon.[5]

Consequently, the varied significance of lithographic prints signals an international relationship that photographs initiate through a wide network of artistic association with Europe at the turn of the nineteenth century. Used by photographers (or companies) as a means of competing with one another and advertising enlargements, reprints, hand-colouring etc., these intricate designs mark the beginning of the growing use of lithography and typology as design tools. Some others prominent photographers showcasing lithographic art identified in the Alkazi Collection of Photography are Johnston & Hoffmann, EOS Studios, S. Hormusji, Shapoor N. Bhedwar, Gobindram & Oodeyram, Lala Deen Dayal & Sons and The Bombay Photographic Co.

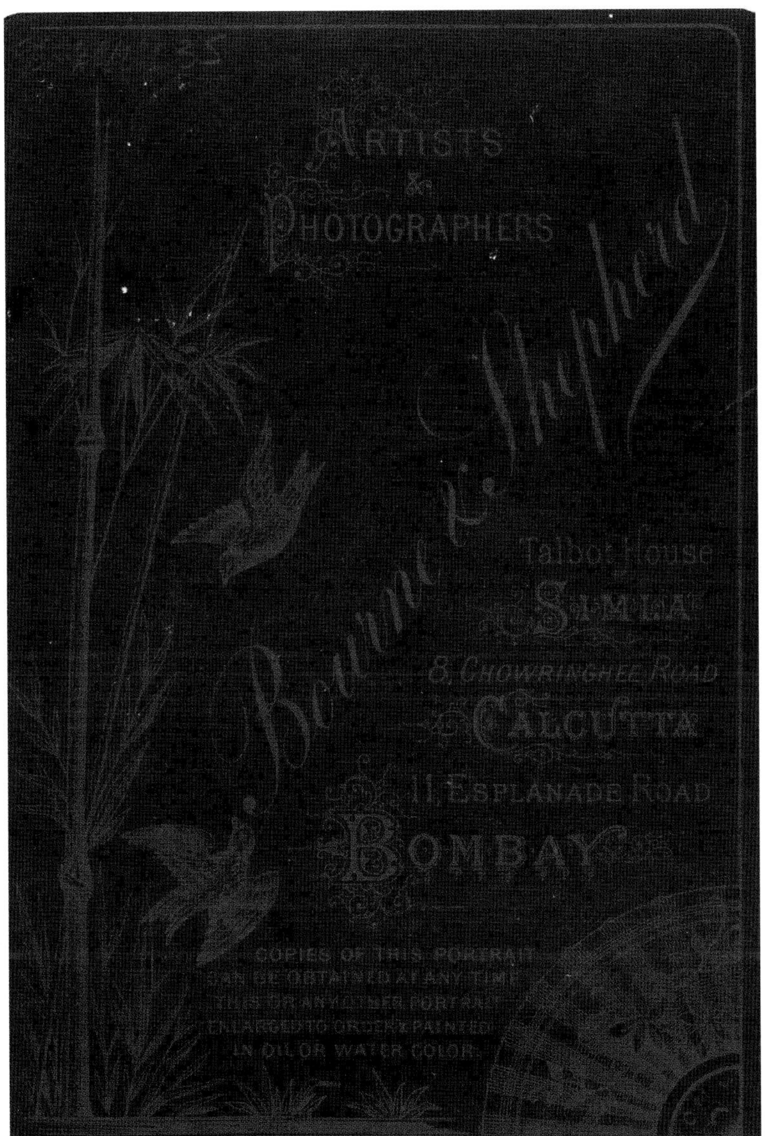


## Select Studio Biographies

### Bourne and Shepherd, Commercial Photographers, Kalbadevi Road

Samuel Bourne (1834–1912) who was a bank clerk took up photography as an amateur, producing accomplished topographical and architectural views. In 1862 he gave up his work at the bank and travelled to India, arriving in January 1863. He reached Shimla, where he set up a studio in partnership with Mr. Howard and later that year, Charles Shepherd of the firm Shepherd & Robertson (q.v.), joined the partnership, creating Howard, Bourne & Shepherd. By 1865 the business had become Bourne & Shepherd (fig. iv). Two additional studios were subsequently established, in Calcutta (1867) and Bombay (later Mumbai) (1870).

[*Reference: Drawn from text by Stephanie Roy Bharat in* Lucknow: City of Illusion, *Prestel and ACP, 2006*]

**Fig. iv | BOURNE & SHEPHERD**
**11, ESPLANADE ROAD, BOMBAY**
Verso of Cabinet Card, 165 x 110mm,
c. 1880–1890s [ACP: 98.60.0035]

## EOS Studio, Kalbadevi Road

Purvezji Dadabhai (1845–1909), founder of the well known EOS studios, was one of the earliest Parsi photographers in Bombay (later Mumbai). Purvezji opened a shop in Bhangwadi, in Kabadevi Road, in 1875, taking photos in the wet-collodion process. In 1883, he partnered with Karl Koening, a German artist and established the "Koening and Purvezji" studio. Soon they bought a larger place on Kalbadevi (fig. v), calling it EOS (after the Greek Goddess of Dawn). Koening left in 1886 upon the death of his wife and Purvez became the sole proprietor. Purvezji died in 1909 at the age of 65 years, and his son and later his grandson carried on the business, which continued till the 1960s.

[Parsi Lustre on Indian Soil, *Vol. 1 (Unknown Binding) by Hormusji Dhunjishaw Darukhanawala, 1938. pp 242–243, gives a comprehensive account of the studio*]

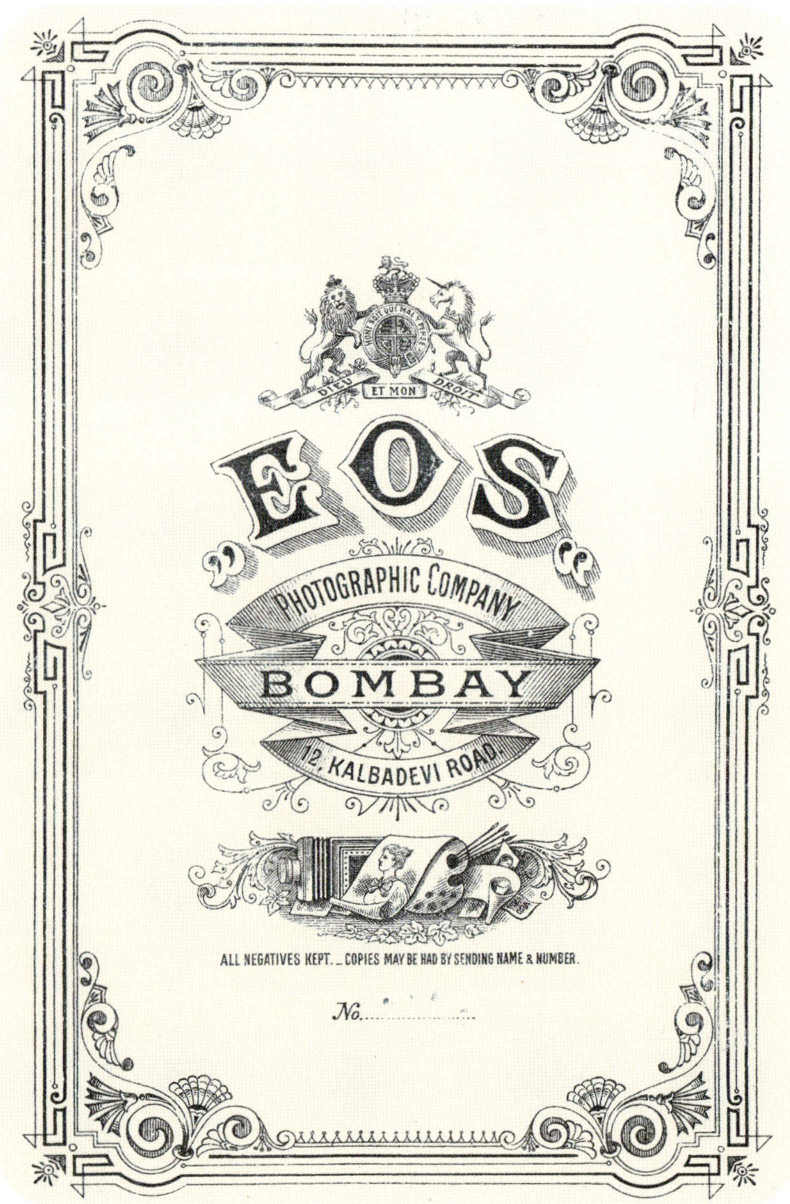


Fig. v | EOS PHOTOGRAPHIC COMPANY, BOMBAY
Verso of Cabinet Card, 164 x 106 mm, c. 1880–1890s
Photographer's Ref. 600a
[ACP: 95.0037 (02)]

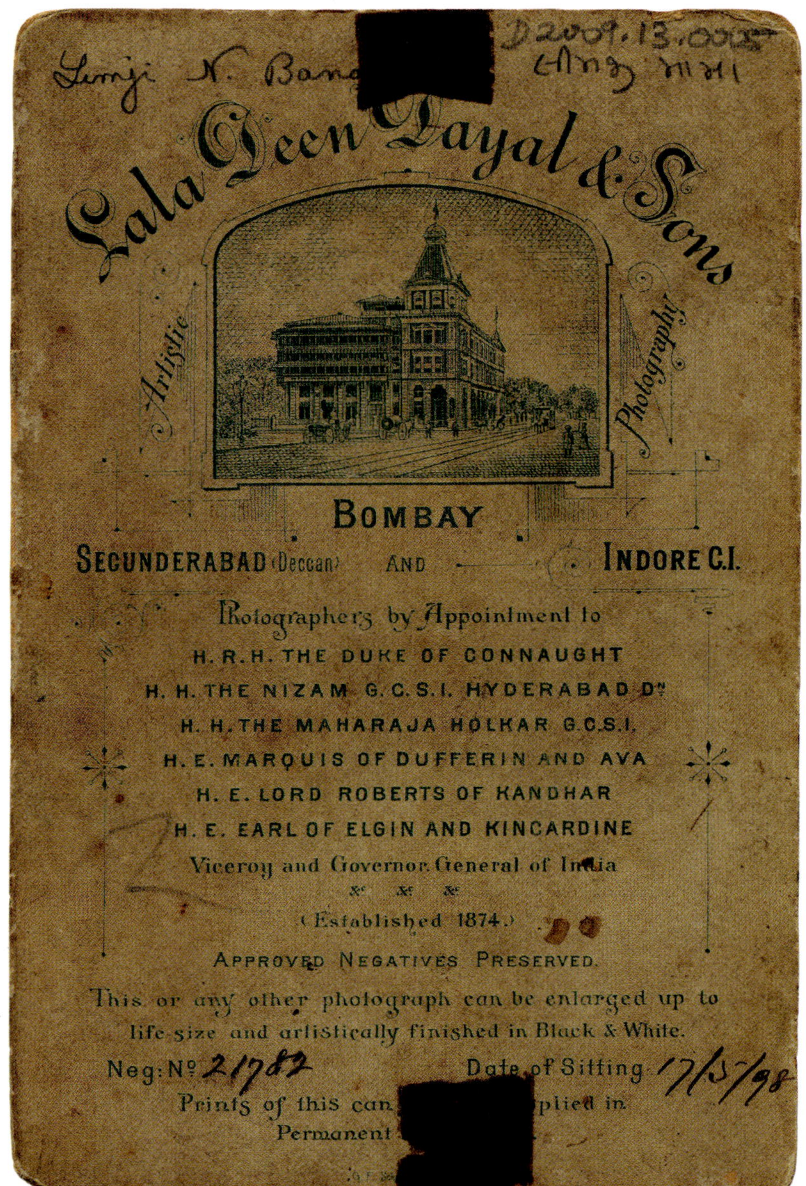


Fig. vi | LALA DEEN DAYAL & SONS, BOMBAY
Verso of Cabinet Card, 165 x 106 mm, 1898
[ACP: D2009.13.0005]

## Lala Deen Dayal Studio, Hornby Road

Deen Dayal, India's premier court photographer, settled in Hyderabad in 1887, where he started a successful studio for the elite and was bestowed with a royal warrant in 1897 by Queen Victoria. The studio opened a branch in 1897 in Bombay (later Mumbai), a spacious facility, styled as "Art Photographic Salon", located on Hornby Road. It contained sixteen rooms, including a large showroom where photographs were on display for visitors and dressing rooms for both gentlemen and ladies. He held an esteemed position not only in the cities where his studios were based, but seemingly all over India. The studio in Bombay closed around 1912 (fig. vi).

[*Reference: Deepali Dewan and Debra Hutton, research conducted for forthcoming ACP publication, 2009*]

## Hamilton Studio, Ballad Estate

Established in 1928 by Sir Victor Sassoon (1881–1961), of the famous Sassoon family, the first photograph taken here was of J.R.D. Tata, who was a patron of the studio. The studio was also assigned the task of photographing the Governors of Mumbai. There were at first 20–25 people, with a strict division of labour between processing, enlarging, colouring etc. Ranjit Madhavji, the current proprietor, took over the establishment in 1958. The studio still exists, with an original posing space and several vintage cameras including an exquisite wooden Eastman Kodak camera from the 1950s. The walls are still covered with portraits of families and officials, some beautifully painted (fig. vii).

[*Based on an interview with Mr. Ranjit Madhavji in December 2009*]

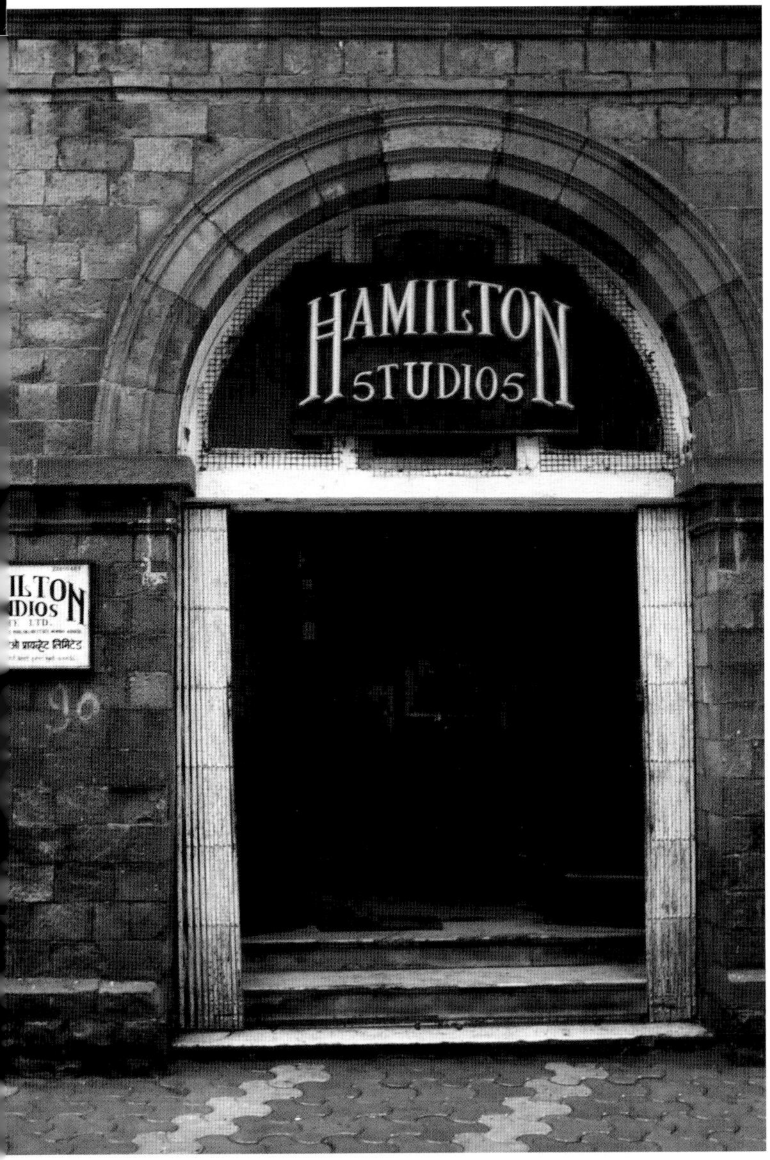


**Fig. vii** | The first photograph taken at **Hamilton Studio** in Ballad Estate, founded in 1928, was of J.R.D. Tata. Photo: Rahaab Allana, 2009

NOTES

1 Referenced in C. Pinney, *The Social History of Indian Photographs* (London: Reaktion Press, 1997) 79.
2 Article in *The Evening News*, 1987, "Close-up of the Oldest Studio" by Staff Reporter, Bombay.
3 William C. Darrah, "Cartes De Visite in 19th Century Photography", Library of Congress Catalogue, Chapter 4: *Portraiture*. No. 81-69489, 1981. 24–25 & 43–45.
4 John Hannavay, *Victorian Photographers at Work* (Shire Publications, 1997) 54–55.
5 William C. Darrah, "Cartes De Visite in 19th Century Photography", Library of Congress Catalogue, Chapter 4: *Portraiture*. No. 81-69489, 1981. 28–29.

## Further Reading


Allana, Nissar. *Painted Sceneries*. New Delhi: Theatre and Television Associates, 2008.

Bajac, Quentin. *The Invention of Photography: The First Fifty Years*. London: Thames & Hudson, 2002.

Baldwin, G. *Looking at Photographs: A Guide to Technical Terms*. California: The J. Paul Getty Museum, 1991.

Bunnell, P.C. "Pictorial Effect". In *The Art of Photography—1839–1989*, edited by Mike Weaver. New Haven and London: Yale University Press, 1989.

Cohn, B.S. "Representing Authority in Victorian India". In *The Invention of Tradition*, edited by E. Hobsbawm and T. Ranger, 165–209. Cambridge: Cambridge University Press, 1983.

Dehejia, Vidya. *India through the Lens: Photography 1840–1911*. Washington DC and Ahmedabad: Freer Gallery of Art and Arthur M. Sackler Gallery in association with Mapin Publishing, 2000.

Enrico, Castelli and Aprile Giovanni. *Divine Lithography*. New Delhi: Eastern Book Corporation, 2005.

Falconer, John and Louise Hide. *Points of View: Capturing the 19th Century in Photographs*. London: British Library Publishing, 2009.

Falconer, John. *A Shifting Focus: Photography in India—1850–1900*. London: The British Library, 1995.

Falconer, John. *India: Pioneering Photographers—1850–1900*. London: British Library, 2001.

Guttman, J.M. *Through Indian Eyes: 19th and 20th Century Photography from India*. New York: Oxford University Press, 1982.

Hannavy, John, ed. *Encyclopedia of Nineteenth-Century Photography*. Vol. 1. New York: Routledge, 2008.

Jain, K. "New Visual Technologies in the Bazaar: Reterritorialisation of the Sacred in Popular Print Culture". *Sarai Reader 2003: Shaping Technologies* (2003): 44–57.

Karlekar, Malavika, ed. *Visualizing Indian Women—1875–1947*. New Delhi: Oxford University Press, 2006.

Mitter, Partha. *Art and Nationalism in Colonial India—1850–1922*. Cambridge: Cambridge University Press, 1994.

Pelizzari, Maria Antonella, ed. *Traces of India: Photography, Architecture and the Politics of Representation—1850–1900*. Montreal: Canadian Centre for Architecture, 2003.

Pinney, Christopher. *Camera Indica: The Social Life of Indian Photographs*. London: Reaktion Books, 1997.

Reed, Martin and Sarah Jones. *Silver Gelatin: A User's Guide To Liquid Photographic Emulsions*. London: Argentum, 2008.

Sinha, Gayatri, ed. "The Colonial Project and the Shifting Gaze". In *Indian Art and Visual Culture—1857–2000*. Mumbai and New Delhi: Marg Publications with National Culture Fund and Bodhi Art, 2009.

Webb, Randall and Martin Reed. *Spirits of Salts: A working guide to old photographic processes*. London: Argentum, 1999.

# Glossary of terms

A selection of processes and formats adopted by photographers of nineteenth century:

***Albumen silver print:*** Invented by Louis-Désiré Blanquart-Evrard (1802–1872) in 1850, it became the most common type of print for the next 40 years. It consisted of a sheet of paper floated in a bath of whisked egg white and salt. Once absorbed and dried, the sheet was sensitized by floating it in a bath of silver nitrate solution and dried in the dark. The sheet was then placed in a hinged back frame, pressed against the negative, either of glass or of waxed paper, and placed in the sun to print, for a time varying between few minutes to an hour. The image was fixed by immersing it in a solution of hyposulfite of soda (hypo) and water, and then washed. The image was often toned with gold chloride to enrich the colours and increase their permanence.

***Carbon print:*** Though invented in 1855 by Alphonso Louis Poitevin (1819–1882), it was patented on April 15 1864 by Englishman Joseph Wilson Swan (1828–1914). The carbon print is a more permanent form of a photographic printing process, as it contains no silver impurities that can deteriorate. Carbon prints exhibit a wide variety of tones, from glossy darks to even cooler shades of grey and blue. Owing to their permanence they were popular between 1870–1910 especially for fine book illustrations and commercial editions of photographs.

***Card photographs:*** These refer to photographs commercially sold in the nineteenth century, which were mounted on to stiff card stock. Of varying sizes, their names depended on the size of the card stock used. Among the more common ones were the *carte-de-visite* (4.5 x 2.5") and the *cabinet card* (6.25 x 4.25"). Other formats included, in ascending order, the Trilby (approx 2 x 2.75"), Victoria, Promenade, Boudoir, and Imperial (7 x 10").

***Daguerreotype:*** The first-known photographic process, from 1839, was the invention of Frenchman Louis-Jacques-Mandé Daguerre (1787–1851). The cumbersome process involved suspending a sheet of copper thinly plated with silver over a container of iodine vapours. The rising iodine vapour combined with the silver to produce a layer of silver iodide, a light sensitive compound. This was then used in a camera and exposed to light for as long as 25 minutes to produce an image. When exposed, developing involved suspending the plate over a container of heated mercury, again, the vapours of which would produce an image formed from an amalgam of silver mercury. The image was then "fixed" or made permanent by immersion in a solution of common salt or hyposulfite of soda and toned with gold chloride to enhance its colour and clarity. As the image is on the plate's surface, it is best seen from an angle to minimize reflections.

***Gelatin silver print:*** Consists of a paper coated with gelatin containing light-sensitive silver salts for making black and white prints from negatives. The silver salt in the emulsion is either silver bromide or silver chloride or a combination of both. With the former, the prints are made by enlargement and with the latter in the emulsion, by contact printing. First invented in 1873 by Peter Mawdsley.

***Wet-collodion process:*** Invented in 1848 by F. Scott Archer (1813–1857), but introduced in 1851, the process gave a higher resolution of detail. It was in use between 1855 and 1881. Collodion was a mixture made from dissolving gun cotton in alcohol, ether and potassium iodide, which was then applied to clean glass plates. The process involved the plate to be sensitized with a solution of silver nitrate while the collodion was still wet, and then placed in a camera for exposure, again while still wet. After exposure, the plate was immediately developed in a solution of pyrogallic and acetic acids though later ferrous sulfate was used as a developer.

***Woodburytype:*** Walter Bentley Woodbury (1834–1885) patented this photomechanical reproduction process in 1864. Just like the carbon process, this too produced prints that did not fade, as the images did not rely on light-sensitive materials. The images were in fact made up entirely of stable pigment suspended in gelatine. Despite the painstaking care required for its production, it was popular till the 1900s because of the high quality of final images produced, which was very true to the original and also highly luminous. Woodburytypes were often pasted into books as illustrations.

*Compiled by Anita M. Jacob and Akshaya Tankha*

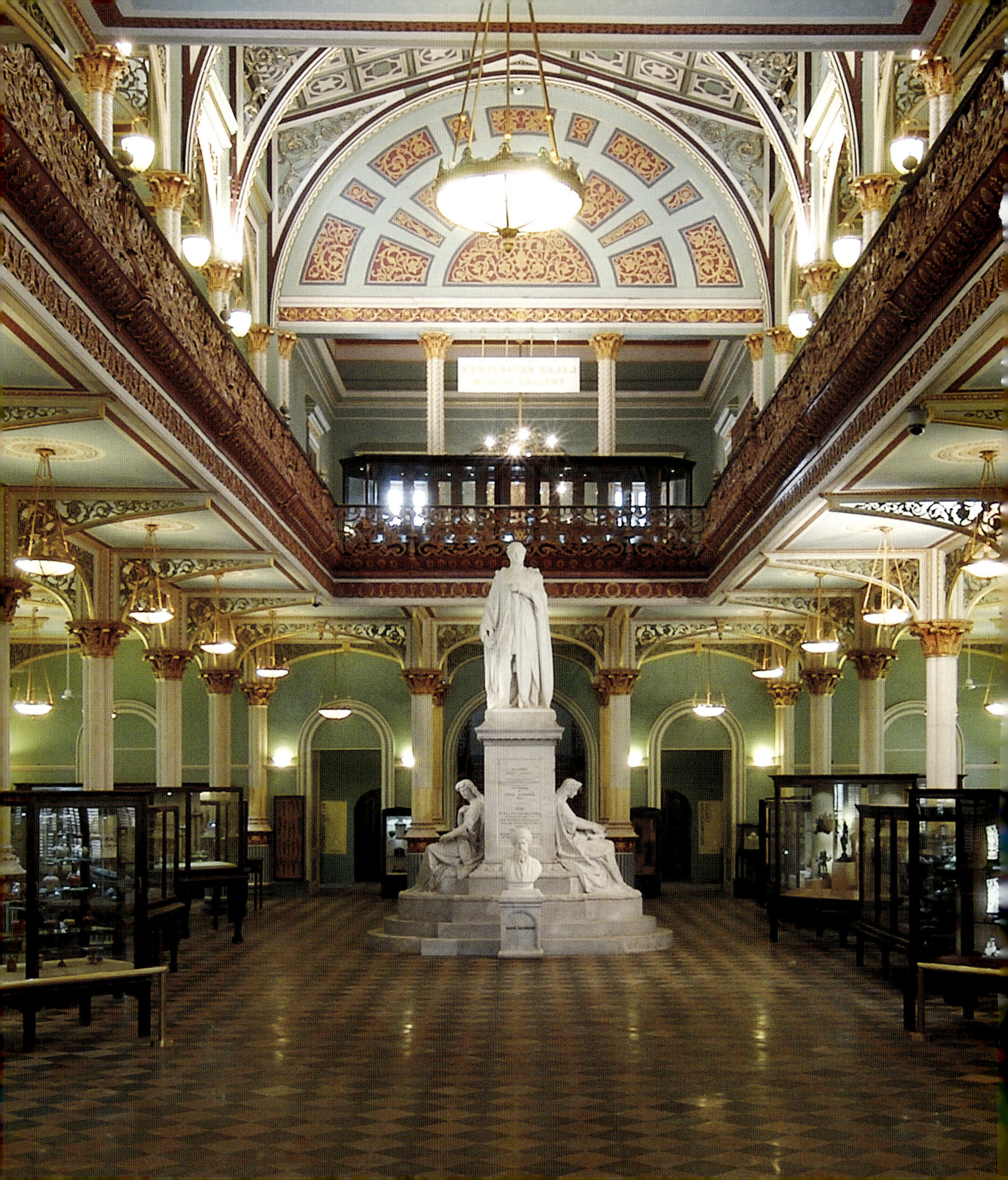
KAMALNAYAN BAJAJ

# Dr. Bhau Daji Lad Mumbai City Museum

The Dr. Bhau Daji Lad Mumbai City Museum opened to public in January 2008 after a five-year long Restoration and Revitalisation Project, which won the UNESCO Asia Pacific Heritage Conservation Award of Excellence, the highest international award for heritage conservation. The Museum was established in 1855 and is the oldest in Mumbai, and the third oldest in the country after the museums in Kolkata and Chennai. When built in 1872, it was named the Victoria & Albert Museum. It was renamed as Dr. Bhau Daji Lad Mumbai City Museum in 1975, under the aegis of the Municipal Corporation of Greater Mumbai (MCGM). The Restoration Project was made possible with a generous donation from the Jamnalal Bajaj Foundation, and with the Municipal Corporation contributing an equal amount. The INTACH (Mumbai Chapter) conceived, curated, designed and executed the project.

The project is a pioneering effort in public–private partnership in the field of culture, and it is the only public–private initiative towards the management of a museum in India. The MCGM established a Management Trust to make the institution autonomous. The Board of Trustees include representatives of the MCGM, the Bajaj Foundation, INTACH, and eminent art historians and citizens of Mumbai. The Mayor of Mumbai is the Chairman and the Municipal Commissioner is the Co-Chairman.

The Museum houses an extraordinary collection of nineteenth and early-twentieth century art from the Bombay Presidency. Beautiful models and dioramas provide extraordinary visual documentation of almost every aspect of life at the time, in the city and the region. It has a large collection of exquisite objects that were manufactured for trade during the latter half of nineteenth century, showcasing the

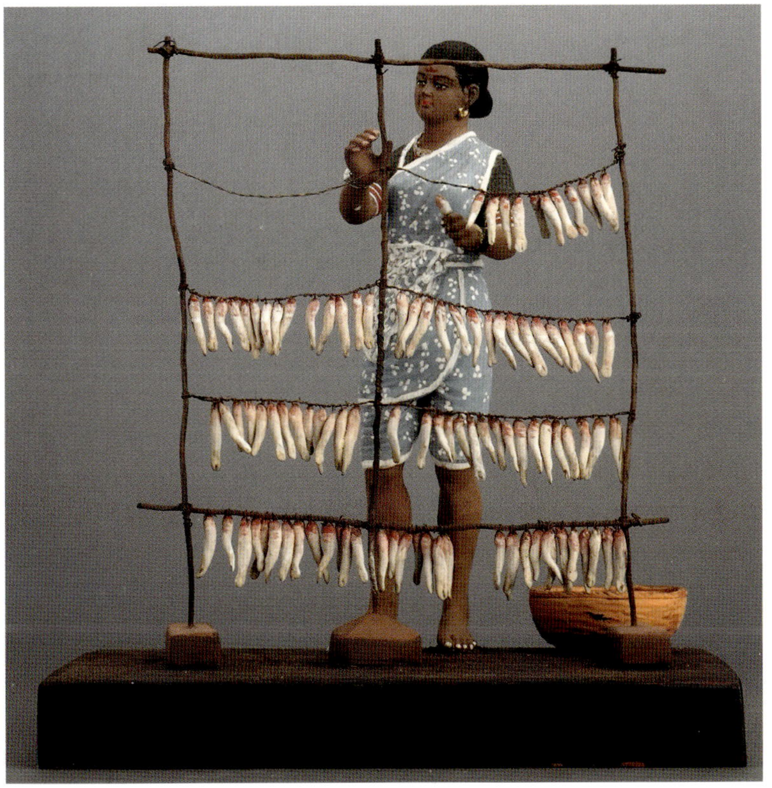

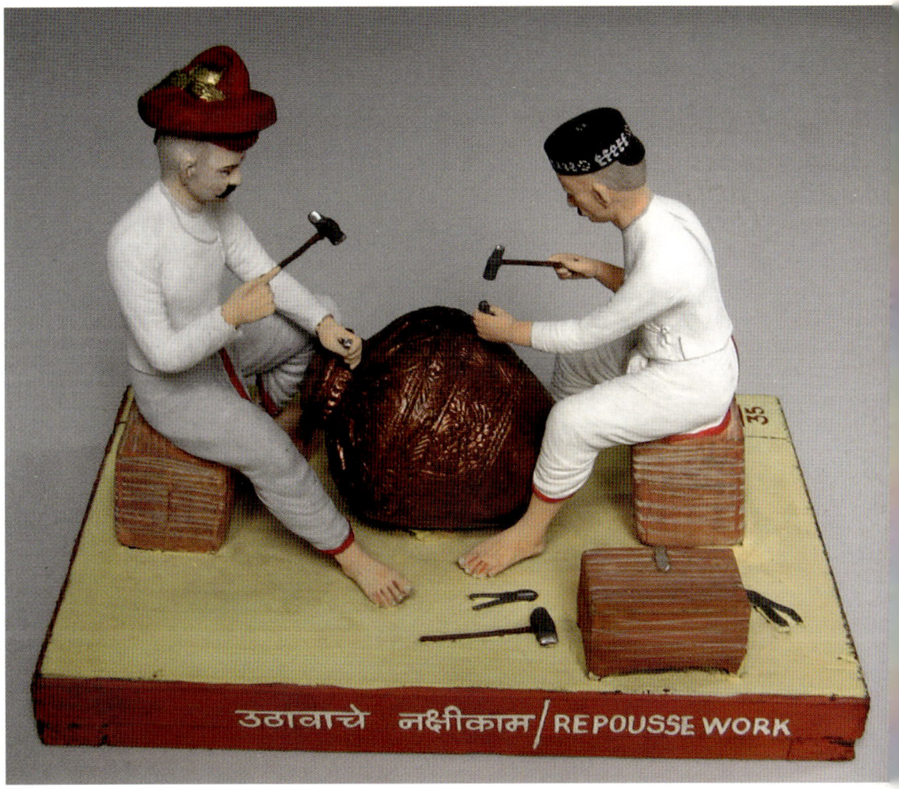

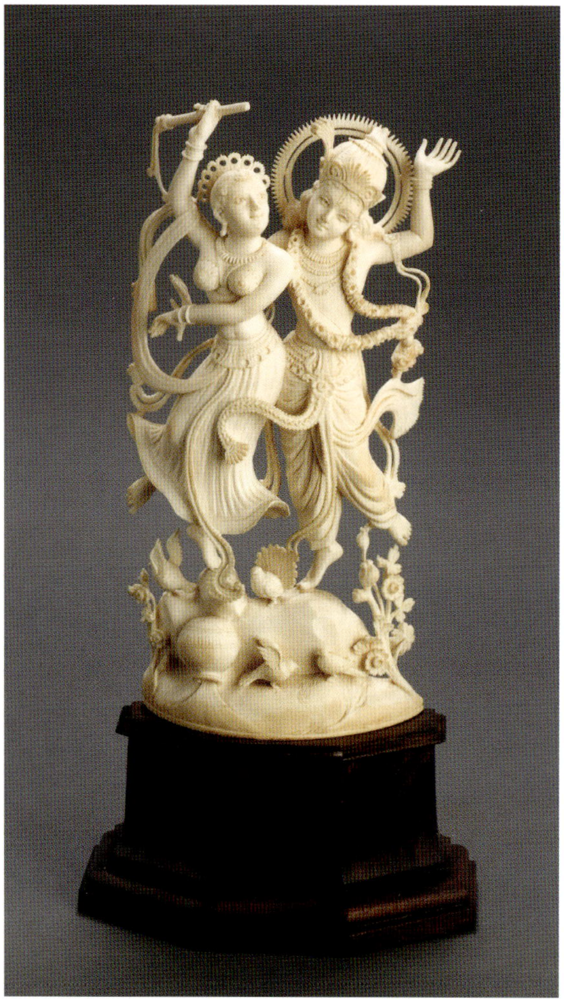

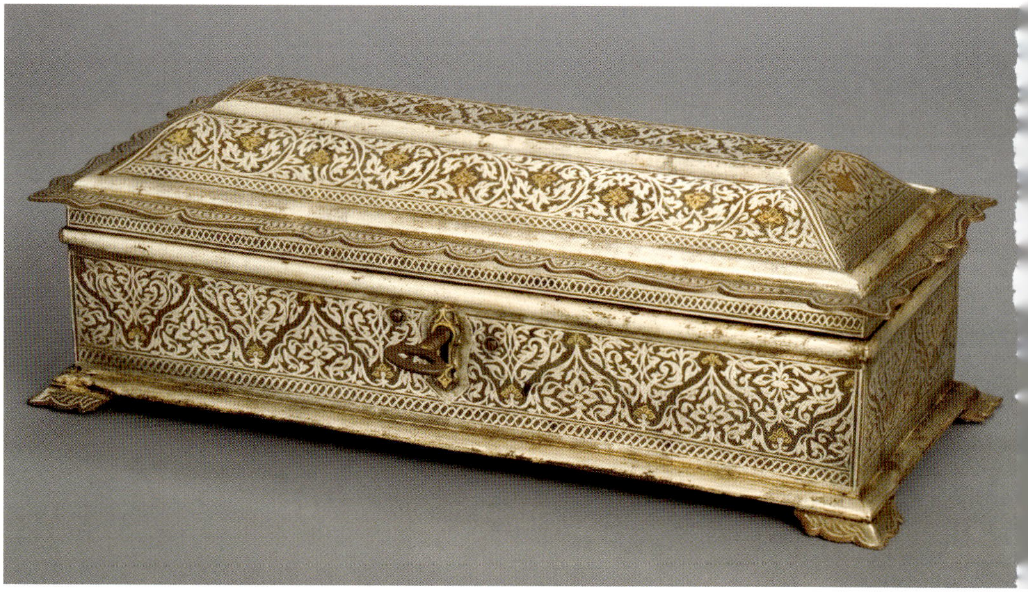

best examples of industrial and decorative design. Many of these were sent to various international Great Exhibitions that were held in London and Europe during this period, and duplicates were housed at the Victoria & Albert Museum in London. Rare books, prints, paintings and maps form an important visual documentation of the city's history. The Museum also has a fine collection of traditional objects such as miniatures and textiles.

The reorganisation of space and the collections has enabled the creation of four separate galleries that focus on different themes. The Kamalnayan Bajaj Mumbai Gallery takes you through the story of Mumbai's origins and development between the eighteenth to early- twentieth centuries. The Kamalnayan Bajaj Special Exhibitions Gallery has been created for special and visiting exhibitions. The Industrial Arts Gallery focuses on the development of design and craftsmanship of trade objects and the influence of the West on indigenous styles. The 19th-Century Paintings Gallery highlights the close relationship between the Museum and the Sir J.J. School of Art that was to forge the beginning of the Modern Art Movement in the city, while the Founders Gallery showcases the story of the extraordinary men who conceived and established the Museum.

The Restoration and Revitalisation Project encapsulates a complete and holistic view of the need to improve and enhance existing cultural institutions to serve a much larger social objective. Along with the building itself, the entire nineteenth and earlytwentienth century collection have been restored, and the display has been comprehensively upgraded. The Museum employs experienced and qualified staff. Extensive exhibition, education and outreach programmes have commenced.

An INTACH Conservation Laboratory and Documentation Centre is set up in the premises, which will continue to care for the Museum's collection. A formal partnership has been established with the Victoria & Albert Museum (V&A) in London. There will be an exchange of expertise and exhibitions, international conferences and seminars on various topics. This programme is supported by the Charles Wallace Fellowship Trust and the V&A, London.

Contact Details

Dr. Bhau Daji Lad Mumbai City Museum
Mumbai
T: +91 22 23731234 / 65560394
E: bdlmuseum@gmail.com | www.bdlmuseum.org

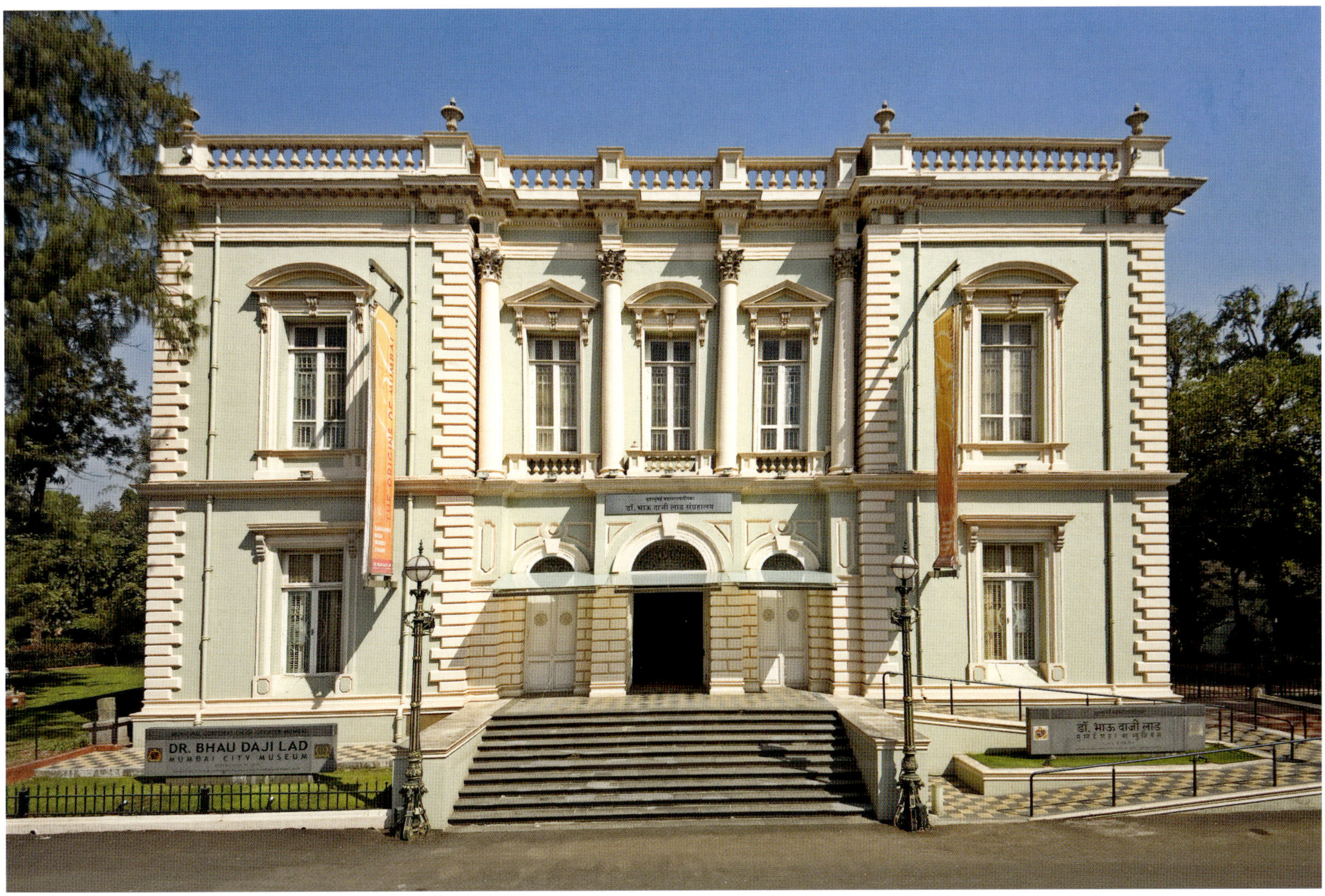

# The Alkazi Foundation for the Arts

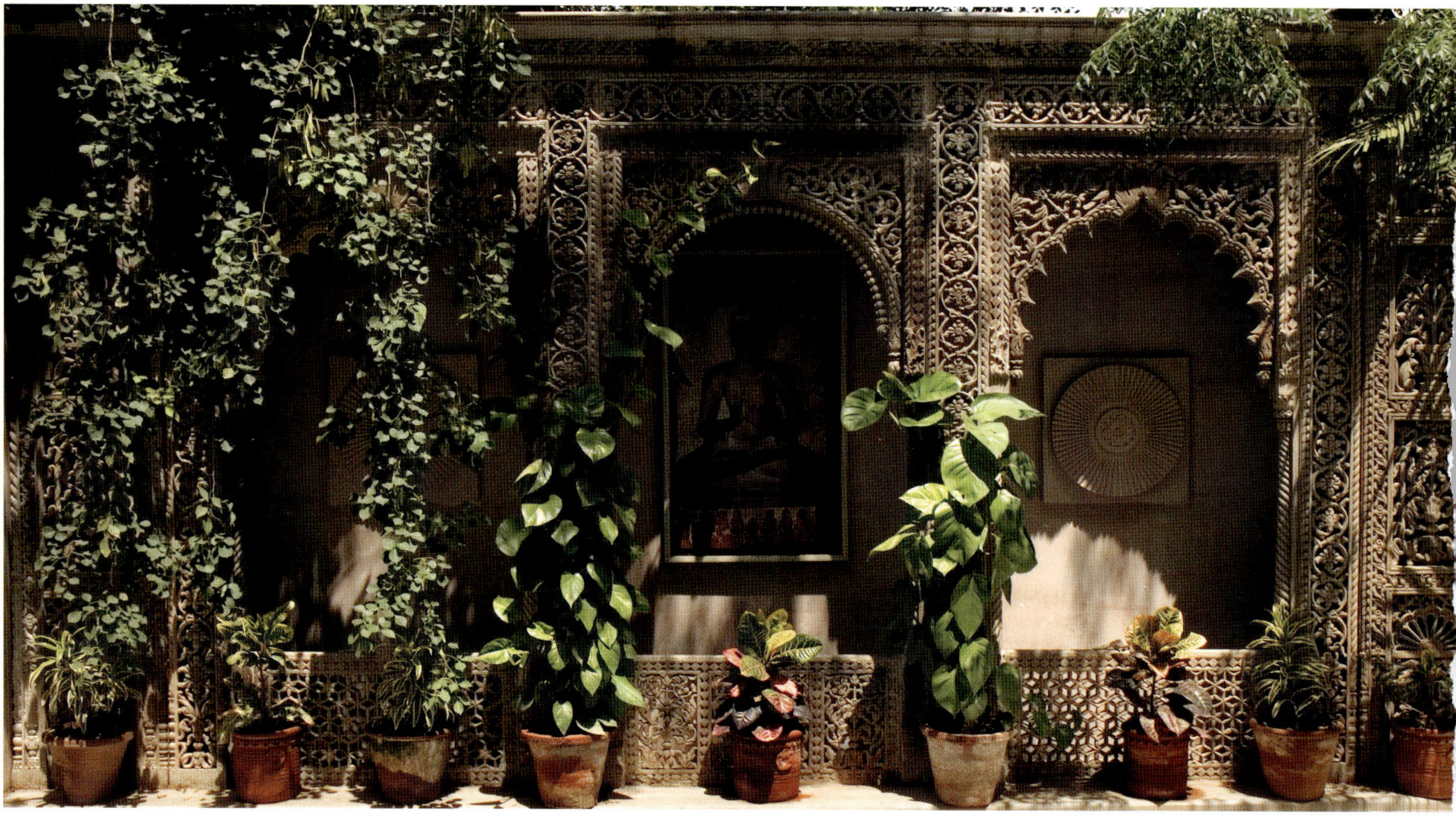

The Alkazi Foundation for the Arts is a registered charitable trust based in New Delhi. Operating collaboratively from its offices in New Delhi, London and New York, the Foundation is primarily dedicated to the exploration and study of the cultural history of India.

## The Alkazi Collection of Photography

Over the last thirty years, Ebrahim Alkazi, the Foundation's Chairman and Director, has amassed a private collection of photographs known as the Alkazi Collection of Photography, an archive of nineteenth- and early twentieth-century photographic prints from South and South-east Asia, amounting to over 90,000 images.

The core of the Collection comprises works in the form of photographic albums, single prints, paper negatives and glass plate negatives from India, Burma [Myanmar], Ceylon [Sri Lanka], Nepal, Afghanistan and Tibet. Almost every region with a history touched by the British Raj is represented. These vintage prints document sociopolitical life in the subcontinent, through the interdisciplinary fields of history, architecture, anthropology, topography and archaeology, beginning from the 1840s and leading up to the rise of modern India and the Independence Movement of 1947. The Collection is particularly strong in the areas of archaeology, architectural history, the urban development of colonial cities,

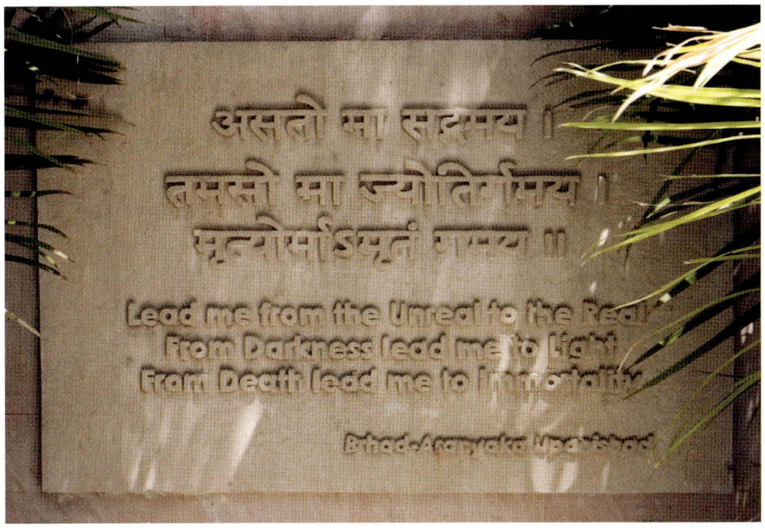


military studies, Princely India and ethnographic portraits of the people of South Asia, as well as landscapes and topographical views.

The proliferation of images points to the early development of commercial photographic studios and the rapid expansion of official photography under the British administration. Prominent photographers featured in the collection include Felice Beato, Linnaeus Tripe, Alexander Greenlaw, James Waterhouse, Samuel Bourne, John Edward Saché and Lala Deen Dayal. The original prints in the Collection have been rendered and archived as high-quality digital images.

In recent years the photographic archive has been catalogued and documented, and is regularly accessed by researchers, curators, historians and teams of scholars. The material is now being made available to the academic community and the general public through a series of publications, accompanied by exhibitions and seminars. Each volume, under the editorship of a specialist in the field, examines a particular region or subject area in the archive, encouraging cross-disciplinary approaches and interpretations.

Contact Details

**The Alkazi Foundation for the Arts**
New Delhi
T: +91 11 41437426 | 27
Chairman: Ebrahim Alkazi
Curator: Rahaab Allana
Consultant: Pramod Kumar K.G.
Research Scholar: Akshaya Tankha
Archivist: Anita M. Jacob
Intern: Jennifer Chowdhry
rahaab@acparchives.com | www.acparchives.com

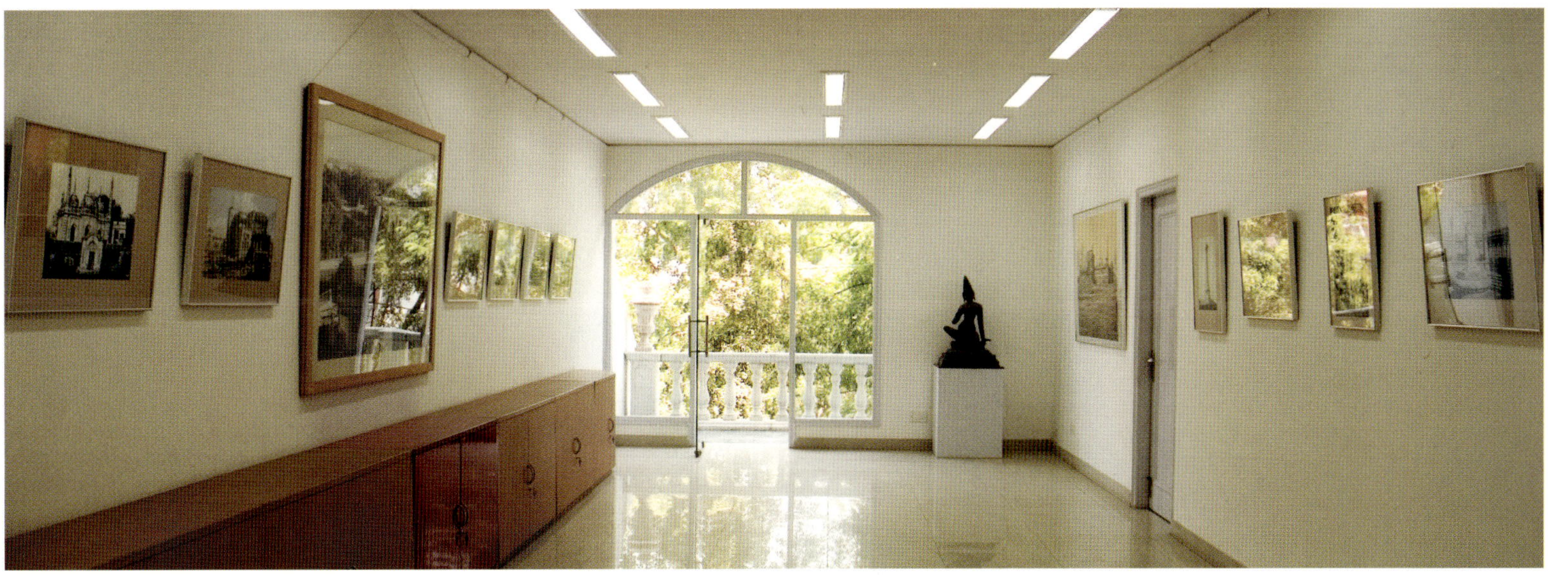

## Acknowledgements

A great number of people have made dedicated contributions to this large-scale exhibition.

This endeavour would never have been possible without the foresight and knowledge of Mr. Ebrahim Alkazi, the master collector, whose private collection of photographs comprise the exhibition; the inspiring determination and energy of Mrs. Tasneem Zakaria Mehta, Director of Dr. Bhau Daji Lad Mumbai City Museum, in collaborating with the Foundation and inviting the exhibition to Mumbai, thereby creating the context for its appraisal by the public.

To the staff members of Dr. Bhau Daji Lad Mumbai City Museum who have worked on the exhibition, we express our appreciation: Alisha Sadikot, curatorial associate, who coordinated the logistics of the exhibition; Bhakti Ishrani Oberoi, graphic designer; Sunil Arya, administration manager; Gargi Mashruwala, finance consultant; Deepti Mulgund, research assistant; and Manoj Pandey, curatorial associate. Poulomi Das , senior assistant curator; Preema John, assistant curator; and Poulomi Sarcar, curatorial assistant, have assisted with the various events associated with the exhibition.

The Alkazi Foundation for Arts would like to thank: Akshaya Tankha, curatorial assistant, for contributing concepts, text and for helping with the final selection of works for the exhibition; Anita Jacob, chief archivist of AFA, for sourcing some hidden wonders from the collection; Pramod Kumar K.G., consultant; Jennifer Chowdhry, intern; Mr. P.L. Dhingra and Mr. Chanda, for administration support.

In addition, we are thankful to:

Mr. Ranjit Madhavji and Ms. Ajita Madhavji from Hamilton Studios

Mr. Rajesh Chaddha from Indian Art Studio

Mr. Sam Maneckshaw for the introduction to Mr. Rustom Vazifdar, who kindly provided detailed information on EOS Photo Studio.

Ms. Gael Newton, Curator, National Gallery of Modern Art in Australia for insights on Shapoor N. Bhedwar

Mrs. Ayesha M. Raza and Mr. Amitabh Srivastav for translation work

Siddhartha Photographix, New Delhi for reprints

SV Photographic, New Delhi for reprography work

COMART for printing banners

Ms. Aadore Sayani for her support

The team at Mapin Publishing

*Rahaab Allana*